Books by Sanaya Roman

Living with Joy: Keys to Personal Powe
Book I of the Earth Life Series

Personal Power through Awareness: A Guidebook for Sensitive People
Book II of the Earth Life Series

Spiritual Growth: Being Your Higher Self
Book III of the Earth Life Series

Books by Sanaya Roman and Duane Packer, Ph.D.

Opening to Channel: How to Connect with Your Guide

Creating Money: Keys to Abundance

OPENING TO CHANNEL

OPENING
TO
CHANNEL

How To Connect With Your Guide

Sanaya Roman and Duane Packer

H J Kramer Inc
Tiburon, California

H J Kramer Inc
P.O. Box 1082
Tiburon, California 94920

Library of Congress Cataloging-in-Publication Data

Roman, Sanaya.
    Opening to channel.

    1. Channeling (Spiritualism)   I. Packer, Duane R.
II. Title.
BF1286.R65   1989   133.9'1   89-2320
ISBN 0-915811-05-7

Cover painting:
"The Third Eye of Harakhte"
©1984 by Judith Cornell

Book design:
Abigail Johnston

Composition:
Curt Chelin

First paperback edition 1987
Manufactured in the United States of America

10   9   8   7   6   5

To all of you Opening to Channel—
for your courage to grow and
your contribution to all of humanity.

To Our Readers
The books we publish are our contribution to an emerging world based on cooperation rather than on competition, on affirmation of the human spirit rather than on self-doubt, and on the certainty that all humanity is connected. Our goal is to touch as many lives as possible with a message of hope for a better world.

Hal and Linda Kramer, Publishers

Acknowledgments

We wish to thank and acknowledge: Our friend LaUna Huffines who we have watched become an excellent channel and who was with us during many of our channelings, for her light, support and ideas; and our friends Ed and Amerinda Alpern for the joy of watching them grow and develop their channeling and for their constant encouragement.

We want to acknowledge and thank our assistants at the Opening to Channel courses: Ed Alpern, Julie Anello, Sandy Chapin, Lynn Crawford, Cindy Haupert, Judy Heckerman, Colleen Hicks, Johanna Holmes, Rhonda Holt, Rikki Kirtzner, JoAnne Marsau, Sue Maywald, Linda Merrill, Patrice Noli, Jill O'Hara, Tom Oliver, Bob Ornelas, Nina Page, Shirley Runco, Vincent Star, Leah Warren, Phillip Weber, and Cheryle Winn.

Special thanks to: Linda Johnston, M.D., Jan Shelley, Wendy Grace, Scott Catamas, Cheryl Willams, Nancy McJunkin, Sandy Hobson, Eva Roza, Mary Beth Braun, Mari Ane Anderson, Mary Pat Mahan, Stacey Mattraw, Michele Abdoo, Evanne Riter, Trudie London, Roberta Heath, Ronnie Rubin, Margo Chandley, Susan Levin, Eve and Lloyd Curtis, Jane Wanger, Loretta Ferrier, Sheila and Earl Babbie, Rob Friedman, and Sally Deutscher.

We thank Georgia Schroer for her wonderful help in managing the office and for her many contributions to LuminEssence and our lives; also thanks to Lois Landau, Sara McJunkin, Adine Thoreen, and Shirley Runco; Denise Laws for tape transcription; Debra Ross for her art and graphics; David Duty; and Jeanie Cragin.

We want to thank the New Age community of Maui, including Romi Fitzpatrick, for their support and wonderful circle of thanks while we were writing the book; the Dallas channeling community, including Jean St. Martin, for their courage in opening to channel and for the support and friends we have found in their beautiful city; and the wonderful people of Mt. Shasta, including Dorothy Kingsland and Missi Gillespie, for their support and encouragement.

Many, many thanks to Hal and Linda Kramer for being so supportive and fun to work with, Greg Armstrong for his editing and suggestions, Elaine Ratner, and Linda Merrill. Many thanks to Abigail Johnston for her imaginative book design, and to Judith Cornell for her magnificent artwork.

We acknowledge all of you who have taken the channeling course for your willingness to be in the forefront of a new consciousness, and we thank you for your stories. We want to acknowledge all of you who will be channeling form this book for your courage and willingness to grow. We welcome your stories also.

We want to thank those who have gone before us, especially Jane Roberts and Edgar Cayce; and all the channels currently putting their work out to the world.

Most of all, thank you Orin and DaBen, who have made this book and this path possible for all of us.

CONTENTS

PREFACE   *1*

Channeling Can Change Your Life
How to Use this Book

INTRODUCTION   *5*

Why Teach Channeling?

SECTION I:
INTRODUCTION TO
CHANNELING

1   WELCOME TO CHANNELING   *13*

What Is Channeling?
What Channeling Will and Will Not Do for You
What You Can Use Your Channeling For
How to Tell if You Are Ready
You May Be More Ready than You Think

2   CHANNELING IN TRANCE   *25*

What Is a Trance State? How Can I Achieve It?
Where You Go When Your Guide Comes In:
   Choosing to Remain Conscious
Our Experiences of Orin and DaBen

3   WHO ARE THE GUIDES?   35

High-Level Guides
Recognizing Entities Who Are Less-Evolved
Personal Guides

4   HOW GUIDES COMMUNICATE
WITH YOU   45

How Guides Transmit Messages
Your Role as Receiver and Translator

5   GETTING READY TO CHANNEL   53

Attracting Your High-Level Guide
What To Expect the First Time
Your Soul or a Guide?
Getting Your Guide's Name

SECTION II: OPENING TO CHANNEL

6   ACHIEVING A TRANCE STATE   65

Guide to Using Exercises
Exercise: Achieving a Relaxed State
Focus—An Element of the Channeling Space
Exercise: Holding a Focus and Concentration
Exercise: Attuning with Life-Force Energy
Exercise: Trance Posture and Position

7   CONNECTING WITH YOUR GUIDE   79

Greetings and Welcome
Process: Ceremony of Welcome to the Guide's Realm
   and First Meeting with Your Guide
Process: Verbally Channeling Your Guide

Questions to Ask Your Guide
   When You First Start Channeling
Instructions for Assisting and Guiding a Partner
   Through First Meeting
Graduation Ceremony—
   Congratulations on Opening to Channel

8   READING FOR OTHERS   97

Giving Readings to Other People
Handling People's Questions
Making Your Readings More Positive
Developing Your Reading Style
Process: Tuning into Another Person

9   PREDICTIONS AND PROBABLE FUTURES   111

How Guides Handle Predictions
How Guides View the Future
Process: Looking into Probable Futures for Yourself
Channeling for Yourself
Process: Giving Yourself a Reading

SECTION III:
STORIES OF OPENING
TO CHANNEL

10   OUR CHANNELING EXPERIENCES   127

Orin's First Appearance
DaBen's Entrance

11   GETTING READY TO
     TEACH CHANNELING   137

Preparing
Putting Up the Bubble of Light
People's Stories: How I Discovered Channeling

12   TEACHING CHANNELING   *143*

Stories of First Meetings with Guides

13   STORIES AFTER OPENING TO CHANNEL   *157*

People's Reactions After Opening
Tecu—Sanaya's Guide from Another Dimension
Our Visit to Mount Shasta

SECTION IV:
DEVELOPING
YOUR CHANNELING

14   CHANNELING—A GREAT AWAKENING   *171*

Channeling—An Accelerated Spiritual Growth Path
Turning Your Doubts into Friends
Is Channeling Just Your Imagination?
Your New Relationship to Your Body

15   STRENGTHENING YOUR CHANNELING   *185*

How Often Do You Channel?
Strengthening the Connection
Receiving More Specific Information
Other Ways Your Guide Reaches You
Will Channeling Help You Win the Lottery?
Can You Change Guides?
Channeling the Same Guide as Others
Can You Lose Your Channeling Ability?

16   GOING OUT TO THE WORLD
       AS A CHANNEL   *197*

Supportive Friends: One Key to Your Success
Your New Role with Friends
How to Talk About Channeling with Others

Going Public
Your Relationship to Other Channels

17 CHANNELING—THE TIME IS NOW   *211*

Channeling in the Past
Channeling—The Time Is Now for Mankind
Find Your Time to Begin

COMPANION BOOKS BY ORIN AND DABEN   *223*

OPENING TO CHANNEL

PREFACE

"Since I started channeling, my heart feels open
most of the time. I am seeing the world in a totally
different way. People seem so much friendlier, and
I feel more willing to be myself. I'm meeting so
many wonderful people; I can't believe how good
life feels."
—*A woman after connecting with her guide*

Channeling Can Change Your Life

This book has a message: Channeling is a skill that can be learned. Channeling involves achieving an expanded state of consciousness that allows you to connect with a high-level guide or your higher or source self. To channel, you do not have to be spiritually evolved or have been psychic all your life; you do need patience, perseverance, and a strong desire to make the connection.

We are encouraging you to be a conscious channel—aware of what your guide says. You will learn how to raise your vibration to sense, see, or hear in the higher realms of the guides, and consciously bring through messages. In the past the words "medium" or "psychic" were used when speaking of contacting guides. This is being replaced by the word "channel." The term "trance channeling" is sometimes used to refer to channeling done in trance; for the purpose of this book we will simply use the word "channeling."

Is channeling real? There are hundreds of stories about scientists trying to disprove paranormal phenomena and then becoming convinced that there was something more to it than met the eye. Many became advocates of channeling or channels them-

1

selves. Although there may be no way to prove whether or not channeling is real in the ordinary sense, we certainly have seen many people use it to produce positive results in their lives.

In the last several years, we and our guides, Orin and DaBen, have taught several hundred people to channel and followed them in the development of their channeling. These people had one thing in common: a strong desire to channel. Invariably, they have reported that it has changed their lives for the better. They say they are able to see a larger picture, to perceive the world in more positive ways. They tell us they have found more compassion for themselves and others. Almost all of them have experienced greater prosperity because of the changes they made in their lives due to new attitudes, a clearer vision of their purpose, and a higher level of trust in their inner messages. People have reported that fulfillment just "seemed to happen" to them. They have felt like they were flowing with the current rather than fighting against it. Piece by piece, people have begun to find their lives taking on a higher order, more meaning, and a sense of purpose. Many have found that channeling is what they were seeking as a major step toward, and vehicle, to enlightenment.

We have seen case after case of enormous personal and spiritual growth after people learned to channel. We have seen not only people's inner lives—their relationships, feelings, and sense of self-worth—grow more positive, but their outer lives as well. Parents became more aware of how to help their children unfold their potentials. Husbands and wives began to communicate on new levels and found deeper bonds developing between them. People found it easier to assist other people, to understand and forgive. They have created places to live, jobs, and careers that were more in alignment with who they were and what they loved to do.

Channeling helps people find their higher direction as well as helping them achieve it. We have not yet discovered limits to the places people can go with channeling, the discoveries that can be made, the information that can be uncovered, or the personal expansion that can be achieved.

Orin and DaBen want to help take the fear and mystery out of channeling. No one we have taught has had a bad experience with a guide. They all followed their intentions to connect with high-level guides. They all used the processes in this book, which were designed to create a safe opening.

We encourage you to use the information in this book as a starting point to assist you in trusting and opening more to your own guidance. Use what fits your experience and discard what does not. Remember, what you are reading is our truth as we have experienced it. If you find you need further information, ask your guide or your higher self and trust the information you receive. The experiences of channeling are so vast that it is impossible to contain them all in one book. More and more about channeling is being written as more of us explore, discover, and play in these higher realms. Honor your own experiences. Stay true to the integrity that is you.

As you open to channel, you are making it easier for others to follow. Be willing to be adventuresome, joyous, and free as you bring in higher and higher levels of wisdom through your Opening to Channel. We welcome you to the wonderful adventure that lies ahead.

How to Use this Book

This book can be used as a course for learning to channel. It is divided into four sections. Section I—Introduction to Channeling (Chapters 1 through 5) gives you background information about channeling—how it will feel, who the guides are, how guides communicate with you, and how to know if you are ready to channel. Section II—Opening to Channel (Chapters 6 through 9) can be used as a course for learning to channel. If you are able to successfully accomplish the first two exercises in Chapter 6 (Achieving a Relaxed State and Maintaining a Focus and Concentration) you could complete the remaining exercises in Chapter 6 and go to Chapter 7 and begin verbally channeling in an afternoon. Proceed at your own pace, completing the course whenever you choose—in an afternoon or over a period of weeks.

Section III—Stories of Opening to Channel (Chapters 10 through 13) tells how we started channeling and stories of some of the people we have taught to channel. The stories illustrate some of the common problems people have as they open to channel and include steps you can take if you encounter these problems yourself. Section IV—Developing Your Channeling (Chapters 14 to 17) gives you Orin's and DaBen's guidance on how to develop your channeling, answers to questions, doubts or fears that may arise, and insights into changes you may experience after opening. These changes include an acceleration of spiritual growth and changes in the physical body. The Appendix gives you suggestions for resources to assist you, including music by others and tape programs and books by Orin.

Sanaya* and Duane

*(pronounced Sah-nay-ah)

INTRODUCTION

Why Teach Channeling?

SANAYA   It was November 23, 1984, the day after Thanksgiving. There was an air of expectancy carried over from the day before when we and some friends at a Thanksgiving celebration had played, channeled, and meditated together. We had all received information through channeling that new things were coming for each of us. Our friends, Ed and Amerinda, had predicted that this was the day their baby would be born. We had all tuned into and shared in this baby's journey into physical incarnation. The theme of the weekend seemed to be birth and rebirth for all of us.

Duane and I had decided to spend time together, to be alone and take a rest from all the classes each of us were teaching and the people we were working with. We planned to take Duane's inflatable boat out on a nearby lake. The weather was fairly warm for a November day in Northern California. We were feeling rested and peaceful, and we decided to channel together before setting out. For the last several months we had been asking our guides, Orin and DaBen, about the higher purpose of our lives.

Orin began innocently enough by telling us about some routine things we might want to pay attention to regarding some personal matters. Then he asked us if we wanted to know how we could truly serve mankind and at the same time align our personal goals with our spiritual paths. Of course we wanted to hear more! Orin began to tell us what was coming for mankind, going on for some time about the changes in the galaxy, the universe, and the

energies that were affecting earth. He discussed the coming vibrational changes and the impact they would have on man's destiny,
telling us how people could discover joy amid all these changes.
Orin would stop at times, and as if on cue, DaBen, Duane's guide,
would take up right where Orin left off, without missing a beat.

In essence they told us that large numbers of people would
be opening to channel in the next five years, and that even more
would feel the impulse to connect with their guides in the next
ten years. They explained that humanity's spiritual self was
awakening, which would result in an accelerated desire for evolution and spiritual growth. They told us that people would need
guidance not only to assist with their spiritual opening, but also
to understand and use the new energies that were becoming
available. A "spiritual shimmer" was being activated in humanity's aura. The ability to reach high levels of consciousness and
find enlightenment was becoming possible for more people.

Orin and DaBen felt that channeling—connecting with a high-
level guide or their higher selves and bringing through verbal
information—would be one of the keys to assist people as they
opened up spiritually. It would help them to make the most of
their new experiences. They proposed that, with their assistance,
we start teaching people to channel. They told us that the theme
of the coming age would be personal empowerment and direct
experience. People would learn to trust their inner guidance, and
many would be opening naturally to channeling. People would
find their teachers coming from within, self-generated and self-
taught, rather than from without. DaBen and Orin wanted to
make sure that people who were opening to channel a guide were
assisted in connecting with high-level guides, that they learned
to recognize high guidance, and that they used their channeling for spiritual purposes.

They suggested we offer a course on channeling. They asked
us to spend the next three months preparing. They would help
by giving us information and guided meditations that would prepare people, as well as processes to use during the course itself.
If we decided to teach channeling, they asked us to make a two-year
year commitment to getting things set up, as it would take that

amount of time for them to put all the pieces in place. After that we could re-evaluate our desire to stay on this path.

At the time, I was teaching the Earth Life courses, a series of spiritual growth courses directed by Orin to help me and those who came to the classes raise our consciousness. In retrospect, I realize that these classes were preparing people to live in the higher energy realms, open their hearts, release negativity, and discover their higher purpose. These skills were good preparation for channeling. Not all people went on to become channels, but many who followed the higher principles began to sense the guides and their own higher selves, and wanted stronger, more conscious connections. The information taught in the courses later became the books *Living with Joy* and *Personal Power through Awareness* by Orin.

Until that day after Thanksgiving, Duane and I had not thought of working together and combining our skills. Yet the more we thought about it, the more natural it seemed. Teaching people to channel seemed like an interesting challenge. Could we do it? Could our guides do it? We knew Orin and DaBen could help individuals connect with their guides and higher selves because both had done so before, but neither Duane nor I had taught a whole group of people to open to channel. Up to this time helping people open to channel had taken months of ongoing work, yet now Orin and DaBen were proposing to open people in a weekend course.

We wondered if they were being too optimistic. We knew many people thought that channeling was difficult and that only a few special people could do it. Some said that it took years of training, or that it only happened to people who had known they were psychic all their lives. Others said that high guides only came to help special people and that it was better not to ask for a high healing master teacher. Orin and DaBen assured us that, because this was a very important transition time for the earth, many high guides were present and wanted very much to assist us. They also said that in the past channeling had required years of special training or had happened only to people who had been born with the gift, and that until recently there weren't as many guides available. Now, for various reasons—the changes in humanity's aura and the vibrational changes of the earth itself—it was possible for many people to connect with a guide and channel.

Orin and DaBen told us that channeling was a skill that could be learned, given the desire and intention to do so. People did not need years of meditation, to be psychic, or to have lived past-lives as channels to do so. They wanted to teach people how to be conscious while channeling a guide, so that people would be able to hear what they were bringing through and have control over which guides they connected with. This way people could hear the higher wisdom of their guides and grow spiritually themselves. They felt that people would be safe by asking and intending to connect with a high guide, or their own higher selves, and by using the processes they provided.

Duane told DaBen he wanted verifiable, provable results for people, or in his words, "I won't do it." He wanted to know that everyone who really wanted to channel could learn to do so, as the guides had said. We spent a month going back and forth. Was it possible? Could we teach many people at once in a weekend course to open their channels, to go upwards and connect with high-level guidance?

Orin and DaBen gave us time to resolve our doubts and questions ourselves before they gave us more directions. They prefer to let us work things out ourselves, to turn to them only when we have exhausted all of our own resources. In our experience guides do not limit individual initiative, but encourage and stimulate it. We decided to teach people to channel and see how it went. Orin and DaBen said it wouldn't take long for people to make the connection, that it was much easier than people thought. They wanted us to help people get through the doorway. As we resolved our own questions the actual processes and course structure came together very easily with Orin and DaBen's guidance. We finally agreed to give the course as often as there were people interested. We never got to the lake to go boating, but our friends did have their baby that day after Thanksgiving. It was a new beginning for all of us.

The first class was a tremendous success. Everyone did learn to channel, and during the next two years we taught several hundred people how to channel in our courses. We are now satisfied that channeling is a skill that can be learned. These people have come from all walks of life and represent many different professions. They have ranged in age from 18 to 70. Just as our guides had claimed, people were able to learn how to channel without years of meditation, prior preparation, psychic experiences, or, in some cases, even much awareness of what channeling was all about. What they had in common was a strong desire to connect with a guide or their higher selves.

People were able to channel and they did so far more easily than they expected. We have kept in touch with many of them and watched them grow and change. They have asked us many questions. They have provided us with insights about their doubts and the challenges, resistances, spiritual awakening, hopes, and dreams that they encountered as they continued channeling. Through their and our own experiences, and with the ongoing guidance of Orin and DaBen, we have discovered much about how to become clear and conscious channels.

Orin and DaBen next told us they wanted to teach people to channel through a book. They wanted us to share all that we had learned and the processes they had given us so that people who were wanting to channel would find guidance readily available. We have shared with you the processes used in the course, especially prepared by Orin and DaBen for this book to connect you with your guide or higher self without the course setting. Their energy is available to you simply by calling upon it. Although we were doubtful at first that people could learn from a book, Orin and DaBen assured us that it was possible. They told us that people's guides and higher selves would help with the connections, and that much help was being provided from the higher realms to make channeling possible for people.

Earlier Orin and DaBen had us put together a book to prepare people for the channeling course, much of which is contained herein. We discovered that people were circulating the book and began to hear of people having spontaneous openings just from reading it. One woman was reading it while flying home. Somewhat skeptically she put the book in her lap, saying, "If you're real, guide—give me your name." From out of nowhere she heard a voice giving her a name, and felt a rush of energy. In that instant she changed her beliefs about channeling and began to pursue a path of connecting with spiritual guides. Many other people have used the processes in this book and connected with their guides and higher selves.

The focus of this book is on how to channel a guide. All of the processes can be used to connect with and channel your higher self as well. If you desire to channel your higher self rather than a guide, ask for this connection as you begin the processes. You may also want to read Orin's book: "Spiritual Growth: Being Your Higher Self" which specifically assists you in connecting with, channeling, and BEING your higher self.

You can learn to channel a high-level guide or your higher self. You can receive guidance, inspiration, and a link to this source wisdom. If you desire this connection, begin now to ask for it. This book is designed to teach you to channel by sharing with you stories, channeled information, and processes. As you continue to read this book, notice the parts that stand out to you, or seem to have special messages. Let these be the first messages to you from your guide or higher self to help you begin your channeling connection.

SECTION I
INTRODUCTION TO CHANNELING

1 WELCOME TO CHANNELING

What Is Channeling?

ORIN AND DABEN   *Welcome to channeling! Opening your channel to the higher realms will create an evolutionary leap for you, for channeling is a powerful means of spiritual unfoldment and conscious transformation. As you channel you build a bridge to the higher realms—a loving, caring, purposeful collective higher consciousness that has been called God, the All-That-Is, or the Universal Mind.*

> **With channeling you can access all the ideas, knowledge, and wisdom that is and ever will be known.**

When you "channel" you access these higher realms by connecting with a high-level guide or your higher self, who steps down this higher vibration and makes it more readily available to you. Channeling involves consciously shifting your mind and mental space in order to achieve an expanded state of consciousness that is called a "trance." To achieve the channeling trance space you will need to learn to concentrate, get your own thoughts out of the way, and become receptive to higher guidance. In this receptive state you become the vessel for bringing through higher energies which you can use for creating good.

You have an innate ability to reach these higher realms; you connect directly with these realms in moments of inspiration, inner guidance, and creativity. You might not be able to reach these realms as easily and as often as you would like. Guides assist you in developing your natural gift to connect to the higher realms. They do so by giving you a boost of energy, providing you with opportunities to grow in new directions, acting as teachers and interpreters, and showing you how to refine your abilities to navigate in the higher dimensions. Guides can help you reach upward in ways that are comfortable and aligned with your higher purpose.

Your guide is a friend who is always there to love, encourage, and support you.

Your guide will encourage and help you to discover your own inner knowingness. As you continue to connect with your guide, you build a stronger, more open and refined, constant connection to the higher realms. You will have more frequent and reliable intuitive insights and experiences of inner guidance or knowingness as the higher vibration flows directly into your mind.

Channeling is a doorway into more love; the higher realms are abundant with love. Channeling is a connection that will stimulate, encourage, and support you. Your guide's goal is to make you more powerful, independent, and confident. The qualities of a perfect relationship—constant love, perfect understanding, and unending compassion—are qualities you will find in your guide.

Channeling will give you the wise teacher you seek, one who comes from within rather than without.

Channeling can provide greater understanding, helping you find answers to such questions as "Why am I here?" and "What is the meaning of life?" Channeling is like climbing to the top of a mountain where the view is expanded. It is a way to discover more about the nature of reality, learn about yourself and others, and see your life from a more all-encompassing perspective, which will help you discover the greater meaning of the situations you are in. Your guide will assist you in finding answers to everything from mundane everyday issues to the most challenging spiritual questions. You can use channeling for healing, teaching, and expanding your creativity in all areas of your life. As you access the higher realms, you can bring through great knowledge, wisdom, inventions, works of art, philosophy, poetry, and discoveries of all kinds.

We, Orin and DaBen, are beings of light. We exist in the higher dimensions, and our goal is to assist you in opening your channel to these dimensions so that you may evolve more rapidly. We have great love for you and it is our concern that you grow and move upward as easily and joyfully as possible. We have put together this course for the purpose of connecting you with your own guide or higher self.

We want to help you understand what channeling is and how you can develop this natural ability. It is easier than you might think, and because it feels so natural, some people have difficulty believing that they have connected with a guide or their source self when they first begin.

The information in this book will help you whether you are thinking about channeling for the first time or have spent years in self-discovery. It will help you learn to discriminate between high-level guides and less-evolved entities, and determine whether or not the advice you receive from a guide is trustworthy. It will show you how to connect with the highest guide possible for you. If you so desire, we want in any way we can to provide you with the opportunity to become a channel yourself.

High guides encourage you to rely on your inner guidance even over their advice.

As you read this book, we encourage you to use only that information which rings true to the deepest part of your being and *discard any information that does not. Trust your inner guidance and messages. You are a special, unique individual with unlimited potential. We invite you to discover more fully your own divinity.*

What Channeling Will and Will Not Do for You

ORIN AND DABEN   *Channeling will assist you in making a difference in the world. This does not mean that you will stop struggling, if you still choose to struggle. It does mean that you can learn ways to do things effortlessly if you choose. It doesn't mean that everything will simply come to you, that you can relax and do nothing. It does mean that you can gain a greater sense of what you want to create and find easier ways to bring it about. If you follow the advice of your guide and continue channeling, changes will occur in your emotional nature and you will less frequently have feelings of depression, anxiety, or heaviness.*

> *High-level guides do not take over or control you.*

Channeling will not solve all of your problems. It will only change you in ways you want to change yourself. You are the one who will make use of the words of wisdom. You are the one who will take action, get the work done and out to the world. You will still be responsible for your life. Channeling is not a cure-all, or an end-all. Channeling, as we have said, simply accelerates your growth opportunities and lessons. You may find yourself re-experiencing and finally clearing up many of the old issues in your life. Although some of these experiences may not be comfortable at first, they will ultimately result in greater joy and power. Be open to small changes. You will find your efforts rewarded beyond your expectations. You may find that even the slightest effort put into following your guide's and your directions will produce great changes and rewards. These rewards won't always be in the form you expect, so be open to pleasant surprises.

*Channeling will help you learn
to love yourself more.*

Channeling does not guarantee that people will love you, nor does it guarantee fame or popularity. Channeling does, however, allow you to understand others in a more compassionate way. You will be able to observe yourself objectively, free of your normal prejudices; this will teach you to love yourself more. Channeling will help amplify and clarify your soul's path. In following your higher path, you may indeed experience fame, recognition, and popularity, but these will not have the same importance as before.

What You Can Use
Your Channeling For

ORIN AND DABEN   *Besides channeling to obtain higher wisdom and personal guidance, some people use channeling for their creative endeavors, such as writing plays, music, or lyrics; and painting, sculpting, ceramics, and handwork of all kinds. Some people's guides assist them in counseling, teaching, therapy, healing, or bodywork. Some use the channeling state and their guide's higher vibration to expand their creativity in acting, directing, and the production of events of all kinds. Each guide and each connection is different, special, and unique. Some guides are poetic, some are inspirational, some are instructive. Some of you may find yourselves able to channel books or write with such ease that books just seem to "get written" for you, for channeling seems ideally suited to writing. Channeling helps you connect to a constant, steady source of inspiration and information.*

Creativity is greatly enhanced by channeling.

Artists tell us that by maintaining a light trance, they can bring in their guides and channel with their eyes open. Their paintings or sculptures seem to appear in visions even before their hands begin to move. Some artists feel that their hands move instinctively to realize the pictures in their minds. Many have felt a slightly altered state of consciousness, in which they were more relaxed and more aware of a richness of impressions that went beyond their normal experiences.

Many musicians find it easier to write music after they learn to channel. They discover a deepening sense of their personal style. Some discover that the state they go into to create their music is a natural channeling state. Connecting to their guides enhances and refines this state, and gives them a more consistent and steady flow of creativity. Some have found that the trance state allows them to flow more with their music, creating it intuitively rather than intellectually. One well-known musician channeled sixteen tracks of music at separate times, and they all fit together perfectly on the first attempt.

People have used their abilities to tune into higher wisdom to discover what exercise, diet, foods, and mental disciplines are best suited to them. We encourage you to discover for yourself all the different ways you can use this connection to the higher realms.

How to Tell If You Are Ready

ORIN AND DABEN *People who become good channels enjoy thinking for themselves, are independent, and like being in control of their lives. The people who become skilled at channeling are often very curious and open-minded. They are aware, sensitive, and in touch with their feelings. They are people who enjoy learning and opening to new skills and knowledge. People involved in creative fields of all kinds are natural channels—writers, healers, therapists, poets, musicians, artists, planners, designers, and so on. People who channel come from all walks of life, from every profession. The qualities most highly valued by the guides are dedication, enthusiasm, and the willingness to be a channel. Those of you who are intelligent or intuitive,* who like to think for yourselves, who value truth, and who can recognize higher wisdom will become very good at channeling. People who channel are kind to other people. They are sincere and hard-working. They become enthusiastic when they get involved in projects. They have vivid imaginations and like to daydream or fantasize. They seem to be able to anticipate other people's needs and care about their families and friends. In relationships they are sometimes unable to distinguish between what is fact and what is fantasy, because they so often see people's potential rather than who they are at present.

Guides will help you achieve new levels of personal power and spiritual growth.

A person who is able to get things done is highly valued. We do not expect your life to be working perfectly, for part of our commitment to you is to help you put your life in order. We expect that making your life work is important to you. We prefer to connect with those who would love our work together so much that they would do it for play. We seek those who are grateful for the opportunity to have this connection.

The highest guides come to those who use and value the information they bring through to the best of their ability. We are interested in people who have spiritual interests, perseverance, and enthusiasm. As high-level guides we are here to make a difference, to serve mankind, and to work with you in a co-creative venture. We take our commitment to you seriously and will do all within our power to assist you. We expect you to also take your commitment and our work together seriously. We highly value those who would give time and energy to our work together, for those are the greatest gifts you offer us.

Having a desire to assist others, and a concern for their well-being also helps in attracting a high-level guide. Channeling always serves others in one way or another, elevating the vibration of the world around you. Any of you who are assisting others in any way—through your business, personal or family lives, or through your creative endeavors—will be able to attract a high-level guide. As you heal and help others to whatever degree you desire, you will also grow.

Do not feel intimidated or doubtful of your ability to attract a high-level guide, for there are many of us and we are here to serve you. We will do all we can to assist you in breaking through to us once you have indicated the desire to do so. We are interested in bringing higher consciousness to mankind, and we will also bring a higher consciousness to you.

People who channel report feeling more grounded, stable, and in charge of their lives.

Some people are afraid that if they learn to channel they will get too "far out" or "spacey" and lose touch with reality. They tell us they already have trouble handling the practical details of their lives and need to be more grounded. We have observed that channeling has helped people feel more grounded, more centered, and more able to deal effectively with their daily lives.

Some people are afraid that if they channel or connect with a guide, they will lose their personal identity or get "swallowed up" by the guide's presence. High-level guides never want to take over your life. Channeling is not a surrender of control. Guides have lives of their own, and their intent is to serve you in your spiritual path. You will keep your own identity, and you are likely to find your sense of self greatly enhanced. You may be able to set limits and define your personal boundaries with others more easily than ever before. Far from being taken over by guides, you will know yourself as a more powerful, balanced, clear-thinking person while they are with you. One man was concerned that he would lose his personal boundaries and be controlled by his guide. After learning to channel, he said that he felt more in control of his life and better able to maintain his integrity than ever before.

Some people are afraid that if they open up they will be vulnerable to negative or lower entities. In actuality you are not vulnerable, for you will easily recognize lower entities by their negativity; all you need do is be firm and ask them to leave. You may also call on us, Orin and DaBen, or any high teacher, such as Christ or your guardian angel. These beings are far more powerful than any lower entity. Once you ask for a high-level guide, this guide will begin to protect you whether or not you are consciously channeling. We only ask and caution you not to play with lower entities out of idle curiosity.

You can connect with a high-level guide.
The only requirements are your desire
and intent to do so.

If you have been interested in metaphysics, if you have been reading channeled, self-help, science fiction, or psychology books, and if you enjoy the ideas you find in them, you have the ability to connect with and channel a high-level guide. If you have been drawn to things which are a step beyond mass thought, if you enjoy being on the leading edge and in the forefront of a movement, then you are ready for channeling. As you begin to channel, the ability to maintain a trance state, focus mentally, good physical health, and emotional stability will contribute to your clarity as a channel and help you to reach the higher levels of wisdom.

Although channeling is of immediate value to you in your life, it takes practice to become good. Those who become adept are people who set aside time to bring through guidance regularly. Just as most people do not become concert pianists in just one session, most of those who develop clear links and good connections to their guides practice on a regular basis.

Ultimately, only you can know if you are ready to channel. Go within and ask, "Do I have a deep desire to channel or connect with my guide? Does there seem to be an inner urge or voice drawing me in this direction?" Listen to your inner messages.

You May Be More Ready than You Think

ORIN AND DABEN *Awareness of your guide usually occurs in stages. During the beginning stages, you may not be consciously aware of your guide. Guidance may come to you in your dreams. You may dream that you are going to school, or you may dream that someone is talking to you in the night, giving you lessons and instructions. You may be asking if you have a guide, or thinking about guides. You may be drawn to books that are channeled by or talk about guides.*

Guides often connect with you in your dreams.

During the first stages of your preparation for channeling, you may start feeling dissatisfied with your life, relationships, or job, and find that you really want your relationships and work to be more meaningful and fulfilling. You will probably desire to find out more about your spiritual path and about what form your life work will take. You may become increasingly aware of your desire to be a teacher or healer, to connect with people in healing and therapeutic ways. You may discover a desire to write, work with the media, play music, or meet new friends. You may feel bored with old friends that you once found stimulating, and some of the social or other activities you used to enjoy may seem less interesting. You may find yourself wanting a higher purpose in your activities, and feeling that spending time without purpose isn't as fun as it once was. You may feel as if something important is coming, that you are in a transition stage. You may be looking for something new but are uncertain what it will be.

You may have reached some of your goals but not felt the satisfaction you expected, and you may be wondering what you could create that would really make you happy. You may already know what your path is and feel a need to experience it in a more concrete or meaningful way. You may be feeling ready to go to a higher consciousness, and want a more open connection to the higher realms.

Channeling will help you discover your higher purpose.

Some people have startling experiences that serve to open them up. Something happens to them that they can't explain rationally, such as a premonition about an event that later comes true, a visit to a new place that seems hauntingly familiar, an out-of-body experience, or a precognitive dream. Others say they feel swept up in something—coincidences start to happen, doors open, books come their way. They start meeting new people and their whole view of reality begins to shift. Some people who have been studying yoga and meditation, explored the Eastern religions, or participated in New Age seminars such as est or Silva Mind Control, find that as they ask, "What next?" they are increasingly drawn to learn more about their healing and channeling abilities. Some people have not even thought much about guides. Then one day they read about guides and channeling, and it suddenly feels right to learn more about it. They feel it will provide them with the shift they have been searching for in all of their previous explorations.

Asking for a guide brings one to you.

As you evolve, your sensitivity to the higher realms increases. Ideas seem to come to you from somewhere beyond yourself. You find yourself knowing things that you didn't know before. You may feel that you are connecting to an energy that is higher than or different from your normal awareness. What is happening is that you are beginning to consciously experience the higher dimensions. If you request a guide to assist you, one will begin to work with you. At this stage the connection to a guide may occur most often in your dream states or in spontaneous or unexpected moments.

You may at some point have a vivid dream in which you are aware that your guide has contacted you. You may discover your connection to your higher self or a guide through Tarot cards, the Ouija board, automatic handwriting, or meditation. During meditation you may begin to get guidance that seems to be of a greater wisdom than what you have experienced before. There are many methods used to initiate the connection. There is no one set way to become ready to channel. Preparation is an individual experience and is different for each person.

Those who are not ready to become channels usually know it, and they are quite clear that channeling is not for them. They may not have the preparation at a soul level. They may not have a world view that encompasses channeling as a possibility. Their skepticism serves to keep them from it until they are ready. It may not be appropriate for them at this stage in their lives, so do not attempt to convince those who are skeptical to try it.

As your connection with your guide and higher self gets stronger, you may think more often about channeling a guide or connecting with your own higher self. You may have had a reading by someone else's guide. You may have gone to hear a channeling, read about someone else's guide, or heard or seen a guide channeled on audio or video tape. Although you may have doubts and questions about channeling, you will find yourself valuing the experience and eager to learn more. If you are ready, thinking about connecting with your guide will bring a sense of anticipation and excitement. Your possible anxiety about it, and wondering whether you have the ability, are indications of its growing importance to you, rather than reflections of your ability to connect with your guide or higher self.

2 CHANNELING IN TRANCE

What Is a Trance State? How Can I Achieve It?

ORIN AND DABEN *A trance state is a state of consciousness that allows you to connect with a guide. There are many ways to describe the experience of the channeling state. Usually, describing it makes it seem more complicated than it actually is. You would have a similar problem describing the state of mind that is required to drive a car, play a musical instrument, or engage in an active sport. Once you have experienced the channeling state, it is easy to remember and return to. Most people find that achieving a channeling state is easier, more subtle, and different than they thought it would be.*

The times when inspiration flows effortlessly are similar to the channeling state.

Most of you have had brief experiences of a channeling-like space, such as talking to a friend in need, feeling wisdom flowing through you and saying things you hadn't originally intended to say. The moments when you feel deep love for a friend, awe as you look at a beautiful sunset, appreciation for the beauty of a flower, or the reverence of deep prayer all contain elements of this state of consciousness. When a very clear internal voice tells you things that seem to come from a higher level than your normal thoughts, when you are teaching others and suddenly feel inspired, when you feel an impulse to say unexpected and wise things or touch in unusual and healing ways, you may be experiencing elements of how a trance state feels.

Trance states feel as if you have suddenly become very wise.

The trance state creates very subtle changes in your perception of reality. Answers to questions may come easily, and they may seem simple or obvious. At first it may even seem as if you are imagining or making up the words and thoughts. You might feel as if you are concentrating. You do not want to push your mind away; actively use it to help you reach higher.

Channeling usually causes a change in your breathing and may initially be accompanied by unusual sensitivity in your upper body. You may feel heat in your hands, or an increase in body temperature. The trance state is an individual experience. For some there is a peculiar absence of physical sensation. After you have channeled for a while, you become accustomed to the accompanying physical sensations, and unusual ones rarely occur. Some people complain that they miss the unusual sensations once they stop. Occasionally, as you reach new levels, there may be a tingling in your neck or at the top of your forehead. Some people feel sensations along the spine or a band of tightness or energy around their foreheads. While channeling, the rhythm and tone of your voice may be different from normal, perhaps much slower and deeper.

SANAYA AND DUANE Various states of consciousness can be related to levels of relaxation and alertness. You are in a number of different states of consciousness every day. Waking and sleeping are familiar and easily recognizable as different states. Different kinds of activities involve distinctive states of consciousness. Your state of awareness is different when you watch a movie, work on a difficult task, drive on the freeway, or participate in a fast moving sport. These states can be identified as different because of variations in alertness, degree of involvement with the environment, level of relaxation or attention, physical sensations, emotions, and the way you think as you engage in these activities.

In their normal waking consciousness, people are very aware of the environment and usually have high levels of internal mind chatter. At this end of the relaxation scale are activities such as thinking, planning, or worrying. As you relax, while listening to music, watching TV, taking a bath, or walking in nature, you may find that your awareness of the environment ranges from semi-alertness to a dreamy state where you are unaware of your surroundings. As you obtain deeper states of relaxation you become less and less aware of your surroundings until you fall asleep.

Channeling involves the achievement of a slightly relaxed state where you can turn your attention inward and upward to receive messages from higher realms. In a light state of relaxation you are usually aware of sound. Sometimes sounds may even seem amplified. At a deeper level of relaxation or during intense concentration, you may feel so absorbed in what you are doing that you become completely unaware of the environment. You may become so deeply engrossed that if someone came into the room unexpectedly you would jump. Still, it is possible to recall information and be aware of sounds in light or deep states of relaxation, so it is better not to judge if you are in trance by how alert or aware you feel.

At first, when you enter into a trance, you may actually become more aware of the environment you are in, particularly when you receive a guide, because you are making a conscious connection and activating your voice. Soon, however, the environment will seem less significant, and you can learn not to let outside noises distract you. Say to yourself, "Any noises I hear will assist me in deepening my trance."

Some experience with meditative states is useful but is not required to channel. The meditative state and the channeling space are both reached from a relaxed state of internal focus; however the ways in which the mind, intention, and spirit are used differ. In deep meditation there is little need to recall and speak, so it is primarily an experience of pictures, energy, and feelings.

Most people who meditate have already begun to access the channeling space. Unless they request a guide, they pass right through the channeling space on their way down to deeper meditative states, and coming up out of these states. They often get their conscious insights during this time. Because channeling is a lighter trance state than deep meditation, it is often easier to achieve than people experienced at meditation might expect. In channeling, you learn to direct your mind to a place—somewhat like finding a doorway—where you link with your guide. While it may take a long time—fifteen minutes or more—to achieve a state of deep meditation, it usually takes a short time—often less than five minutes—to achieve a channeling state.

When you reach up into the channeling space your guide joins you and helps direct your energies. Channeling does not require a calm, still mind, like meditative states, but instead requires the ability to concentrate and focus. Getting into a channeling state isn't just up to you. You will receive a lot of assistance from your guide in achieving this state, because you have asked for the connection and guidance.

Where You Go When Your Guide Comes In: Choosing to Remain Conscious

ORIN AND DABEN *Some people set aside their waking consciousnesses entirely when they channel. They say channeling is like falling asleep, and remember nothing of what is said. Those whose conscious awareness disappears during channeling are called "unconscious channels." These unconscious channels usually enter into such deep states of relaxation that they have no recall of their guides' messages. They are usually receiving the energy of the transmissions, if not the actual words of advice at a soul level, but are unable to recall what their guides have* said. Your recall will vary depending on the nature of your trance state.

Some channels remain partially conscious, and, because they can remember some of the transmission, they are called "conscious channels." These people are aware to varying degrees of the information as it comes through. Some may have vague senses of their guides' messages, but little memory of what specifically transpired. Some compare it to remembering dreams since their memories fade very rapidly afterwards. They might remember the information just as they come out of trance, but are unable to remember it an hour later. Some channels have very light trances, remember what is said, and feel very alert during channeling. The experiences of most people fall somewhere between deep, unconscious trances and fully alert states.

We suggest that you remain conscious while you channel. If you find yourself falling asleep or going under, use your will to stay alert. It will help if you are well rested. There is nothing wrong with being unconscious during trance, but if you are conscious you are able to bring the higher wisdom and light of your guide directly into your own awareness and consciously use the information to learn and grow. We encourage you to be aware to some degree of what you are saying while you are in trance.

Conscious channels are partially aware of what is being said by their guides.

Those who remember what transpires during their channeling generally feel a great richness that surpasses the actual meaning of the words. They feel as if they are in expanded states of consciousness where every word has greater meaning than they have been previously aware of. Sometimes the words are accompanied by feelings of traveling. Sometimes they have feelings of internal shifts to higher vibrations. Some say that channeling is like being in vivid dreams, full of action, emotion, and often color. After coming out of trance this richness begins to fade. Some say that they feel a part of other realms. They feel themselves expanded physically, feeling larger than normal. Some say they feel that normal words become pictures which are translated into richer and more complete internal languages. Some feel as if whole "balls" of information are dropped into their minds, containing complete packages of ideas which they slowly unravel as they speak the messages.

Those who have become skilled at taking their waking consciousnesses into deep levels of trance report that, contrary to being "knocked out" or unaware, so much happens that it is as if they are experiencing the thought impulses of their guides directly. It may seem like being actively conscious during a dream. These thought impulses, in the universal language of light, convey experiences, pictures, and impressions that are far beyond the capacity of your language to express. Those who are fully conscious are aware to varying degrees of the richness of energy beyond words as they experience their guide's world and their own simultaneously.

In conscious channeling, you may find yourself in a slightly disassociated state, one in which you are aware of what is going on, though not interfering with it. Many people say that it is as if they can observe their lives from two perspectives simultaneously: their guide's and their own.

> Conscious channeling involves raising
> your vibration to sense, see, or hear
> in the guide's realms.

There are many, many variations on the experience of channeling. There are many reasons why some people remember their channeling and others do not. Some people do not want to be unconscious or taken over and want to be aware of everything coming through them. Some people are naturally deep level trance subjects. They may want to learn to stay conscious during channeling to avoid drifting into unconsciousness.

It is a rich experience to get your personality, thoughts, and feelings out of the way, and to be conscious when your guide *is speaking. Some people think they are really channeling a guide only if they are unconscious, but most channels are aware to some degree of what they are saying. Lack of any awareness is much less common. Many great and well-known channels described different degrees of consciousness while their guides were speaking or writing through them.*

If you would like to experience an element of the trance state at this time, go on to Chapter 6 and do the following exercises: Achieving a Relaxed State and Holding a Focus and Concentration.

Our Experiences of Orin and DaBen

SANAYA   I experience Orin as a very loving, wise, gentle being with a distinct presence. He has wisdom and perspective, as well as a breadth of knowledge, that exceed anything I consciously know. There is a richness of impressions that goes beyond any of the words that he is saying. While I am conscious, I am not able to affect the words as they come through me. I can stop them, but I can't add my own words or change the message. A week before he gives me dictation on a book, I can feel him organizing the ideas and I become aware of bits and pieces of them floating into my consciousness. Once Orin has decided to teach a class on a topic, I'll receive information on the topic at unexpected times, usually when I run or meditate or when I happen to be thinking about the topic or class.

When I channel, I receive many pictures, feelings, and images, and I can hear my own thoughts and comments alongside Orin's. When Orin leaves, my memory of what he said fades like a dream. I can remember the general ideas to some degree, particularly if they have an impact on me personally, but I cannot remember the details of the information unless I read it afterward. I seem to be more aware of the thought or concept, the overall direction, than the individual sentences. Unless the information is discussed afterward I remember little of what Orin said. However, when I bring Orin through again he can remember exactly what he told people—even years later.

My experience of trance varies, depending upon the information I am bringing through. I go into a very deep trance when channeling information for books and relaying esoteric information of universal knowledge. When I am channeling for other people, my trance is lighter, for it does not take the same amount of Orin's energy to transmit this kind of information.

DUANE   Receiving transmissions from DaBen changes greatly, depending on the type of question and person asking the question. The most challenging questions for me to accurately transmit answers for are those that lead to "scientific" explanations from DaBen. Questions relating to life-force or the nature of reality will lead DaBen to send me images of wave patterns which I must then decipher. These patterns challenge me to pick my own words and concepts to convey their meaning. When DaBen channels guided meditations, I experience his energy being directed outward to those listening. When the channeling is over, people often report that they felt as though they were taken on a tour of some higher reality or that they feel much better and more expansive than they did before. When he channels general information for people about their lives or on various personal topics, I remember very little of what is said, though I am aware of the general flow.

I experience DaBen as a very radiant energy, loving and exacting, who has great caring. His knowledge is very detailed and extensive. Some of the information is so complex that he has been assisting me in developing new words to transmit it. He does not want me to gloss over his concepts or simplify them, even when people cannot immediately understand them. Sometimes I understand them myself only later, after I have put several scientific channelings together and seen the interactions between them. Often I have to consult my physics books to understand what he might be explaining.

I experience fairly light trances when I am working with touch on people's energy systems, particularly because I need to move around and retain awareness of my physical surroundings. My trances are much deeper when I am channeling general information and when DaBen leads people into various experiences of expanded consciousness.

Although DaBen will search for specific information about a person's life in response to questions, it is clear that he prefers to work directly with their energy. Through my touch or by transmitting energy to them, he helps people achieve higher energy states where they can answer their questions themselves.

When I finish channeling I can remember the concepts that were gone over as though my mind is working in a new way. The specifics, however, fade very quickly. When I read the transcripts of the channelings I am amazed at how much more information is contained in them than I remember channeling. It's as if I remember only a few of the hundreds of ideas that are compressed into the words used.

3 WHO ARE THE GUIDES?

High-Level Guides

ORIN AND DABEN *There are so many places that guides come from that they appear to be infinite. You might find it useful to classify guides into those who have been incarnated on the earth and lived at least one earth life; those who have not lived an earth life and are from dimensions outside the galaxy and stars, such as the fourth dimension; the Masters, such as St. Germain; Angels, such as Michael and Raphael, including guardian angels; and extraterrestrial entities from other galaxies and planets. There are other guides that do not fit into these categories. I, Orin, have lived one earth life very long ago in your years, so that I could better understand physical existence. I have long since evolved into pure light and spirit, having no physical body. DaBen is also a being of light and has not lived an earth life.*

Your guide chooses you to work with because of a similarity of goals and purposes.

Not all entities from the higher realms choose to be guides, just as not all of you choose to be channels. Work on the other planes of reality is as varied as your work can be on earth. Guides are certain beings who are highly skilled at transmitting energy from their dimension into yours. It takes an enormous amount of energy from our plane to reach through to yours, and it is done most often out of pure love of humanity and devotion to transmitting higher ideals. As you reach the higher realms altruistic service to others is a path of rapid evolution. We pick you because of an alignment of goals and because we love you.

When we speak to you, others in our realm may help to amplify our energy, for our substance is so fine it takes focus and amplification to reach through to you. Our vibrations are so expanded and vast that to narrow it to frequencies that can be held in your mind takes much practice, skill, and intent. We adjust our perceptual processes to accommodate to your different concepts and understanding. To make a connection with you we must be able to work with energy and our electromagnetic fields at very subtle and refined levels. There are different levels of proficiency in this ability.

You will hear of the causal plane if you are exploring metaphysics. The causal plane is a very high, fine vibratory dimension that you can exist in after this life only when you have harmonized many of your energies and evolved to a high state. Most souls exist in the astral plane when they die, for they are not yet evolved enough to live in the causal plane. Many high guides come from the causal plane and beyond, from what is called the "multidimensional" reality. To live in these other dimensions requires mastery of the polarities, an advanced level of control over the emotions and mind, and skill at using energy. Some guides have lived on earth, evolved quickly, mastered the lessons, are now pure spirit in the causal plane, and are evolving further through serving humanity. Others come from the multidimensional realities and are extremely high beings in their own systems.

Some of you may choose to channel your higher selves. Your higher self can provide love, compassion, spiritual guidance, and wise counsel. Both your guide and higher self are here to serve your growth, boost you higher, and assist you in living your higher purpose.

Guides can appear to your inner eye as particular nationalities with clothing that is appropriate. I, Orin, appear to Sanaya as a radiant shimmer of light that sits around her body when she channels. She is aware that I am about eight or nine feet tall. All that she can see whenever she tries to see my face is brilliant white light. I often appear in robes such as your ancient monks wore.

Some report seeing their guides as color. Some perceive their guides as sounds, others feel their guides as openings in their hearts. As you become accustomed to seeing in the higher vibrational planes, some of you will be able to see your guides more clearly. Some people picture their guides as familiar figures they have known, such as Christ, Buddha, or angels, who represent great love and wisdom to them. Guides can appear as American Indians, Chinese sages, East Indian masters, or as one of the Great Masters, such as St. Germain.

Guides may appear as either male or female, although in the realms of pure energy there is no polarity, so guides are not truly male or female. Guides will choose an identity that will best accomplish what they are here to do, or one that you can most relate to. If by the nature of their work they want to embody such qualities as softness or nurturing, they may take on a feminine appearance. Often a guide who wants to represent a masculine role will take on a masculine appearance. Some will adopt the appearance of a previous life if they have lived one on earth, and use the name of that person. There are as many identities for guides as there are for people, so be open to whatever form or appearance your guide presents him or herself to you in.

Some guides are purely intellectual and want to impart new ideas of science, logic, math, or new systems of thought. Some entities from other dimensions are from the worlds of essence beyond all form. They are appropriate to be channeled by people who are not concerned with the forms, details, or specifics of their lives or work, but want to work with energy directly, or in ways that involve experiences of energy essence. If you are looking for specific advice from these guides about where to live or what business choices to make, you may be disappointed. However, if you want to work with energy through touch or bodywork, they may help you produce amazing results. If you want to learn about the nature of reality, they may be able to give you lengthy explanations.

Even at the highest levels, guides have different talents and areas of expertise, just as you do. Some may be very good at giving concrete advice, problem solving, and helping you out with your everyday life. Some may be good at giving inspiring, informative talks or relaying spiritual truths. If you ask a question about a subject that is outside their speciality, they will find the information and get it to you. For instance, your guide may be quite adept at channeling spiritual information, but he might not have information about scientific matters. If you need scientific information for something, and it is important for you to have it, your guide will get it to you—perhaps by sending a book or a person with the knowledge your way—or it will come from another guide.

Don't think that once you channel you must be able to do everything. Guides pick you because you are most aligned with what they want to bring to earth. So most likely, what you have been wanting to do or are already doing with your life will continue to be developed with the help of your guide. Let it be all right if there are areas outside your or your guide's realm of knowledge.

Some guides are called "beings of light" because they work with light and use the language of light.

Many high-level guides are nearly pure energy, having evolved into spirit and taken on the shimmer of light. Some could be called "beings of light" because they work in the spectrum of light and use the language of light, transmitting thought impulses directly into the souls of those they work with. We, Orin and DaBen, are beings of light. We are able to navigate the fourth dimension as well as the fifth and higher dimensions. We have evolved beyond the causal plane and come from what you call your multidimensional reality. Our assistance is available when you call on us or your own guide. Our goal is to assist you in linking with your own guide from our realms or a guide of comparable wisdom and light to help you evolve and achieve higher consciousness.

There are so many places where guides come from that it is more useful not to worry about where they are from but to differentiate between guides who are working for your good and guides who are not. Souls of all levels of mastery can exist in every dimension. Entities can be from many different dimensions and realities, and be at different stages in their own evolutions; it is important for you to be discriminating about what guide you connect with. Great teachers exist in every plane of reality. We are primarily concerned that your guide is sufficiently skilled and able and committed to assist you with your spiritual growth.

High-level guides are sources of guidance, clarity, and direction.

People often ask us, "How can you tell if the guide you attract is a high-level guide?" We think that all of you have the ability to recognize a guide who is not high. When you meet people, you have an immediate sense of how wise and loving they are. You know if you feel good and happy around them or depreciated and unhappy. With a guide, use the same faculty of judgment that you use with people. You have the ability to recognize wisdom. Truth feels as if you already know it.

High guides come to light your path. Their only wish is for your higher good. They are there to help you with such things as remembering who you are, letting go of fear, and learning to love yourself and others. They come to add to your joy and to assist you with your personal growth and your work here on earth.

High-level guides neither frighten you nor build up your ego. They do not flatter, although they will applaud your progress. They create a sense of expanded awareness and greater inner vision. They encourage you to use your own wisdom and discernment rather than blindly follow anything you are told. They never tell you that you "have to" do something or attempt to determine a direct outcome in your personal life. They support and encourage you to develop and use your inner strengths and deeper wisdom. They will encourage you not to give your power to them.

High-level guides are often humble, and acknowledge that their truth is not the only truth. They may make strong suggestions and assist you in making your own choices. High-level guides may point out something that is not working in your life, but they will do so in such a way that will make you feel empowered and strong.

High-level guides rarely predict future events. If they do, it is only because the information is useful for your growth or for mankind. If the information you receive from someone else's guide diminishes you or makes you feel bad about yourself, choose if you want to accept it as your truth or not. If you come away from a reading by a guide and you feel fearful about your life, then you have not been with a high-level guide, for they leave you feeling uplifted and supported in who you are. They help you see yourself in new and expanded ways. Be aware that you can turn an uplifting message into one of less joy if you choose to hear it as negative rather than positive.

High-level guides have your higher purpose as their main concern.

High-level guides express themselves with precision, and say much in a few words. They teach tolerance and encourage forgiveness. Their advice is practical, often simple, modest, never boastful, and follows good sense. Any steps they advise are useful and bring greater good to a person's life. High-level guides speak only good about people and things, for their whole nature is filled with love and goodness.

If you ask, they will show you your lessons, speak to you of what you are here to learn, yet allow you to continue in a situation if you choose. They are careful not to take away your lessons. If you are headed towards something that will teach you a valuable, but difficult, lesson, they may show you more joyful ways to learn the same thing. However, if you persist in your original way they will not stop you. It is up to you to choose joy, but if you learn best through pain and struggle high guides will not take them away.

Recognizing Entities
Who Are Less-Evolved

ORIN AND DABEN *There is sometimes confusion about whether or not to follow the advice of a particular guide. It is up to you to use your own ability to discriminate and recognize wisdom. When you receive advice from your guide or from someone else's guide, ask yourself, "Is it appropriate for me to follow this information? Does the information limit me or expand me? Is it accurate? Does it have practical value for me, and is it immediately useful? Does it feel like my inner truth?" Remember the last time you got advice from a friend or guide that didn't turn out well. Wasn't it true that there was a part of you that didn't want to follow the advice? You generally know what is best for you. Weigh the information you receive carefully. Use your common sense to decide whether to use the information or not; don't just blindly accept information about your life. High-level guidance will assist you in having greater confidence in your own truth. Channeled advice is to be followed only if it rings true to you, not just because it is channeled. Do only those things that feel joyful or right to you.*

> *Only accept those messages
> which ring true to the
> deepest part of your being.*

How do you recognize entities who are less-evolved? Some of them love to give predictions of a disastrous nature, and enjoy the heightened emotions such as fright that they can stir up in people. Their predictions are not made to assist people or given with a higher purpose in mind. Their messages may falsely build up people's egos by telling them they are going to be rich or famous when that is clearly not part of their path. You will know if you are connected with a lower guide. You will feel scared, powerless, depressed, or worried about your life after they have given you advice.

Less-evolved entities may want to incite you to take action that you know is not high and loving. Entities who are less-evolved often stir up bad feelings between friends, trying to get you to take revenge. They may suggest that you protect yourself against some frightening and unseen dangers. Some entities, particularly less-evolved entities, thrive on your intense emotions and will try to bring them out in you. Other entities simply waste your time and give you inaccurate or inconsequential information. Lesser entities speak with pretension, in trivialities, or say things in a way that seems to be profound but actually says nothing of value.

Lower-level guides may have no commitment to bringing your energy to a higher order. They may be uninterested in your spiritual growth; they may not even have an awareness of paths which lead to spiritual growth. They may not have a consciousness of mankind's current evolutionary direction. You will recognize this because the guidance they give you may sound interesting but will have no practical value to you. They may not be bad entities, but they may not share your goals or purposes or understand your unique destiny, and thus, might not be able to "guide" you. These entities will probably not be injurious to you in any way, although you might experience some discomfort being around their negativity. They may even be loving in their intent, but may not have achieved any higher evolution than you have. You will know if they are less-evolved by their lack of greater understanding and wisdom.

There is a level of reality one frequency or step removed from yours called the "astral plane," where many souls go in between earth lifetimes. In the lower levels of the astral plane, there are many entities who want to come back to earth. They might want to experience life through you. They usually don't have a bad intent, only ignorance. You can recognize them as they come closer because you may feel their emotional fears, pain, and uncertainty. You will feel their lack of peace. Most souls in this level are not evolved enough to help you and we recommend that you not channel these entities. They represent a cross section of humanity from all walks of life. These earthbound entities may not know they have died. If you sense this is the case, tell them to go to the light.

Guides will speak through you only with your permission.

We recommend that you never bring these beings into your body or verbally channel them. You will know them because their vibration and feeling are not high. You will feel heavy or even resistant to them. They will not take you over because the earth realm is very difficult for them to penetrate. You are the one in control of this reality. Your curiosity, your willingness to play with them or humor them will keep them around. Be firm and sever the link. Guides will not deceive you if you ask them where they are from. If you ask them if they are from the light they will not say "yes" if they aren't. Ask for a high guide and one will be there.

A high-level guide will help you feel more compassion for yourself and others.

If entities other than high and loving guides want to talk through you, simply tell them "no" firmly and clearly. As you channel your guide, you will know what he or she feels like. It will be impossible for another being to fool you. A high-level guide will feel uplifting, loving, and wonderful. You will experience a sense of well-being. If in any way you feel depressed, sad, or angry, then you are not with a high-level guide. Ask that guide to leave and request a higher guide.

Personal Guides

ORIN AND DABEN *Everyone has a personal guide who is with them for a lifetime, often referred to as a guardian angel. Sometimes there are several guides helping you, particularly if you are at a major turning point in your life. Usually, these personal guides are less-evolved than the high-level guides. They are more highly evolved than you because they have usually gone through life on earth, and are aware of a greater reality than you are. They can be people you have known in your lifetime who are no longer alive and have evolved beyond earth-based negative emotions. They can be beings whom you have been with in other lifetimes.*

They are here to help you follow your chosen destiny and to help oversee specific issues, and they will work with you whether or not you stick to your highest path or are even aware of them. Part of their purpose is to help you accomplish what you came here to do. These guides are not "less than" high-level guides, but their span of dimensions and consciousness is not as broad or as all-encompassing as those of high-level master guides.

High-level guides work with your personal guide to help you with detailed and specific information about your personal life. Personal guides act as links between you and your high-level guide in certain areas. Once you connect with a high-level guide, most of your conscious connection with your personal guide will be through the high-level guide, not directly to your personal guide.

SANAYA AND DUANE   In dealing with guides the possibilities seem to be truly infinite, and what you experience about guides may be different from what we have experienced. We encourage you to honor your experiences with guides. Let your guides tell you about who they are and where they are from, and don't try to make them fit into any category. The information from Orin and DaBen is not a set of rules, only guidelines.

4 HOW GUIDES COMMUNICATE WITH YOU

How Guides Transmit Messages

ORIN AND DABEN *Guides make contact with your soul, and their information then flows through your soul to your consciousness, translated through the words and concepts that you have available. There are an infinite number of ways a guide may transmit information to your soul. The trance state and focus help clear away personality distortions to create a clear "channel" for the information to flow through.*

To channel, you step up your frequency as you achieve a trance state, and we lower ours to match. It is not an exact energy match, but a complementary one. We create electromagnetic fields in our dimension that are similar to yours in your dimension. As we align both of our energy fields, transmission can take place. Our ability to "match" your frequencies for accurate transmission is also important. As you continue to channel we learn by feedback how to monitor our transmissions and to control the electromagnetic fields. You learn how to track our fields more accurately as you become more experienced at channeling. We also give you immediate boosts of energy when you are going into trance.

To help you understand this extremely complex matter, imagine that there is only one universe. Think of us not as existing in a universe apart from yours, but in the same universe at a different frequency. We are invisible to you until you alter or expand your consciousness so that you can receive our thought-impulses.

We are aware of each and every one of you reaching upward.

We can come through you only when we set up frequencies that can match yours and thus open the doorway. We only see and hear you when we adjust our frequencies in a way that makes your universe visible to us. When you reach upward, asking for a guide, you change your energy and become visible to us. Your intent to go higher is very visible in our universe, and we are aware of you as you reach upward. Even when you become visible, we usually do not see you as you see each other. We perceive you as moving energy patterns, colors and harmonies. We perceive your world as moving harmonics of energy and life-force. When you request a connection to us, we begin to set up matching frequencies in our dimensions to make it possible.

We guides view your earth reality as the three-dimensional world. The higher the dimension, the fewer the limitations or obstructions. When you die, you increase your frequency in such a way as to be invisible to the earth plane, but visible to other realities. You become able to walk through walls or physical matter. It is not the density of the walls that make them impassable for you now, but the relationship of your vibration to theirs. As you increase your vibration, things that were invisible to you before become visible, and obstructions, such as walls, become transparent to you.

Channeling is a skill that can be learned.

Your brain is physically composed of right and left sides. Normally, the right side of your brain deals with intuition, feelings, nonverbal communication, creativity, and inspiration. The left side of your brain uses memory, logic, words, and language. It functions to synthesize, organize, and categorize your experiences in a rational way. Most often, guides transmit to the right side of your brain, which is more receptive and sensitive to impressions. Channeling requires establishment of a particular type of flow and a synchronization between both sides of the brain. This is accomplished in the calmer, more peaceful trance states, allowing greater receptivity to the higher realms.

Channeling requires using your right-brain and left-brain simultaneously. Part of the challenge of receiving a guide is to let go, to learn to receive the higher flow of information (a right-brain function) and, at the same time, speak or write (left-brain functions involving action, organization, and vocabulary). Using your left- and right-brain simultaneously makes it possible for the messages of the guide to be transmitted with precision and accuracy.

As you channel, new pathways through the neurons of your mind are being laid, developed, and utilized, creating a change from your normal mode of thinking. Every time you learn a new skill such as typing or drawing, new neural messages and pathways in your muscles are developed from your arms to your brain. Every time you bring in more light through channeling, you will think in higher and more focused ways, even when you aren't channeling.

In conscious channeling the guide impresses the message upon your mind through what might be called higher telepathy. This is the kind of reception we are encouraging, where you retain control of your muscles. Some people "know" the message (called clairsentient), some "see" the information (clairvoyant), and some people "hear" the information (clairaudient). Some receive the transmission as a richness of impressions that they then match with words.

Some guides transmit to you using a form of higher telepathy.

As in all telepathy, general ideas can be transmitted more readily than specific images such as names, dates, and details. To develop *the skill of getting specific details often requires a long period of attunement with your guide. We often transmit light-images, thought-impulses, and energy level data and allow you to fill in the substance, action, and exact words that most closely matches the energy transmission we are sending. Many transmissions are best sent as pictures and images, and then must be translated into words using your vocabulary and conceptual framework.*

Some guides talk in metaphor and stories with illustrative examples. Some guides work directly on blocked energy. Some guides work with color, shape, and form. Some guides speak through your throat or use your hands for creative endeavors. Some guides talk about energy centers, some about past lives. Some talk about the soul's purpose and some discuss the higher truths of the universe. Some are poetic, others philosophical, humorous, or serious. Occasionally guides challenge people through a series of direct questions to find their own answers, rather than giving them information.

Guides will choose a channel with a vocabulary or skill that will be a match for their work together. Scientific guides may choose channels with a scientific vocabulary. Artistic guides may choose artists. Philosophical guides may choose channels interested in philosophy, and so on. When guides transmit information outside of your vocabulary, they will search for the closest words you have available. For instance, in referring to an organ in the body, they may give a description of it rather than calling it by name, if you don't have the term in your vocabulary.

Guides use your words and concepts to express their messages.

Sometimes when you connect with your guide, words will come instantly to mind. Sometimes you may simply feel the words forming and speak, without prior knowledge of what you are going to say. One man reported seeing the words just before he spoke as if they were coming out of a typewriter. He simply read the message as it was typed. Others see a screen with images un-

folding, and then speak about or interpret the images. Guides will use whatever method is most suited to you and the information at that moment. Messages do not always come through your voice. They can come in any way in which you can express yourself, such as sending energy through your hands in a touch. Guides will choose the easiest way to get their messages through. You will receive the information in whatever way feels the most natural to you. The method of transmission may change as you continue to channel.

Your Role as Receiver and Translator

ORIN AND DABEN   Since you are the one who speaks, you might view your role as that of a translator. You may have a "feeling" about the correctness of your translation of the transmission or a "feeling" of what to say. You may "feel" the right word in preference over the not quite right word. To improve your accuracy as a translator, pay attention to how you feel. If you suddenly feel uncomfortable, let go of what you were channeling and let another direction emerge. Slow down, and pay attention to the words coming through. We will signal you through a discordant note or feeling if you have chosen an inappropriate word or concept.

If you find yourself becoming bored with your information, then it is a sign that you have lost the connection to your guide. Sometimes you'll find yourself talking and notice the original impulse from your guide that was behind your words is gone. If you find yourself filling in words, slow down and speak very slowly. That will allow you time to compare the right feeling of the words with the flow of energy that is being sent through you.

After a channeling session, we may also signal how you may improve your reception. You may find yourself thinking back on what you transmitted, reflecting on how you could have spoken more accurately, with more compassion, or with a more positive feeling. Your concern will reflect our attempts to improve transmission.

It usually takes practice to receive your guide's messages clearly.

Your guide has to get used to your energy systems and make fine and subtle adjustments. Even though sometimes the words and concepts will seem as if they come from your mind, they will be elevated to a higher vibration, and be spoken and framed in a different way. Perhaps the hardest messages to channel are those that are obvious, or those that convey the answers you expected. Sometimes it is harder to channel for those you love or know well because a part of you may already know the answer, and if your guide says the same thing, you may think it is coming from you rather than the guide. Most channels we have worked with convey the messages exactly as they receive them with the greatest sincerity. If you receive something that agrees with what you already know, don't invalidate the message.

Not all transmissions will have perfectly matching forms or words, or even concepts. There is usually something lost in translation. Any of you who are translators have already experienced the difficulty in putting the words of one language into the words of another; different languages reflect different processes of thought. As you begin to channel, we notice what words, phrases, or concepts you select to match our transmission. We are able to observe your personality, your beliefs, and conceptual frameworks, and adjust our thought-impulses accordingly. We monitor your translation closely and constantly fine-tune our transmissions, so that your reception is a better and better reflection of the essence of what we are sending you.

At times you may feel that you're remembering and talking about a past experience of your own as you channel, and it seems to fit right in with the reading. It might feel as if you are using your memory rather than channeling a guide. Your guide might have you talk about an experience you just had, although it will seem as if you are talking about it from a higher level of wisdom and understanding.

*Anything you do that expands your awareness
will help you become a better channel.*

All the reading and exploring you have done will increase the
resources you have available for your guide. Your guide will use
ideas that you have read about and synthesize them in a new way.
He may take an idea you read about ten years ago, or use
something you just learned yesterday. Realize that anything that
is in your mind is a potential tool for your guide.

When your guide is talking to someone, he or she may speak
to you in your mind: "Remember when you read this book.
Remember this paragraph, remember this concept." This may be
exactly what the person you are giving a reading to needs to know
at this point. Your guide may go through your mind and select
something within your memory that is appropriate for you to say
at that moment. Another kind of transmission is to give you a
"trigger" word. You might start by receiving the word "courage."
As you speak that word, a whole association of thoughts and ideas
then come to you, all triggered by that one word.

Your guide will translate your personal wisdom into a more
general framework. He or she will show you the universal lessons
you are learning through your experiences and help you to view
your own life in a higher, more spiritual way. Your guide may use
these universal truths for others, also.

*Guides encourage you
to connect with your own soul's wisdom.*

To trigger your voice, we normally use your thoughts. When
you are channeling, we are the undercurrent beneath your
thoughts, the part that selects which thoughts to trigger, that
causes your mind to speak of certain things, in a particular way.
We light up certain areas of your mind, and we also trigger your
own soul's knowledge. We draw not our ideas, but the words

necessary to express them from your mind. The richer your mind is with knowledge and experience, the more words we have to choose from to express our thought-impulses.

Your guide is going to come through your personality and your voice, so he or she will feel a lot like you in the beginning. Remember, since you are used to thinking your voice is you, when you hear it as your guide speaks you will associate this sound with your self speaking. It is often easier to believe that it is really your guide speaking if your guide sounds different—has an accent, different pacing, or tone than your normal voice.

Language is very important, and precision often becomes a matter of the size of the picture you comprehend. We would have to write volumes to explain the basics for you to understand many of our concepts. In shortening the message to assist you, some of the precision and accuracy is lost, and there is the possibility of misunderstanding. We walk on a fine edge, simplifying our messages, keeping them understandable to you, while, at the same time, preserving the depth, the clarity, the wisdom, and the truth as they exist at our level.

Often we convey our messages by using examples, metaphors, and comparisons. In this process, there is always the possibility of oversimplification. Exceptions or special instances are not always included. We may need to create words to explain what we mean, for often no words exist in your vocabulary. As you grow and understand more, we can convey more complex messages to you or messages of a broader scope. We give you the advice you can use and understand in the present. Sometimes you draw the wrong conclusions from our advice because you didn't see the larger picture. Information you receive about a topic at one stage of your growth will usually be expanded, clarified, and modified as you grow. This is why it is valuable to record and reread what you have channeled. As you look back from a future date when you are aware of a bigger picture, you can often see an interpretation of the information different from the one you saw originally. You may see a greater wisdom in your guide's message than you originally suspected; the message may be more profound and meaningful when seen from a future date.

5 GETTING READY TO CHANNEL

Attracting Your High-Level Guide

ORIN AND DABEN *Your first meeting with a guide is a special time, and it is best to prepare for it as a special event. It is a unique experience, different for each person. Even those who have been receiving indications of the presence of a guide, find that the actual time when the final adjustments are being made, right before they make the first full connection, is charged with anticipation.*

The actual invitation and entry of a guide into your life may take place in many ways. It can happen under the supervision or direction of another high-level guide, or you can contact your guide yourself by asking for the connection. We have designed this book for you to show you how to contact your guide. The processes in Section II, Chapters 6 and 7, can be used as a course for calling in your guide. You can do the course by yourself or with the assistance of a friend. Another easy way to do the course is to make tapes for yourself, using the processes in Chapters 6 and 7 as guidelines to assist you. If you would like, you can also use the audio cassette tapes that we have made to prepare yourself for opening to channel and to assist you in calling in your guide. (See Appendix for tape programs.)

Another easy way to start is to have a friend present who can ask questions, hold a focus, believe in you, listen, and assist. Some people find it easier to channel when someone else needs assistance or an answer, for the desire to help others will often stimulate them to overcome their hesitancy to speak or make the connection. We have provided instructions for having a friend support you in Chapter 7.

At some point you may want to channel with someone else present, since the responses of another person give your guide additional feedback about the level and complexity of the information he can present. As you and your friends express your understanding of the message, your guide can more fully evaluate how you are translating the messages and adjust the transmission accordingly. Your guide can then decide whether the messages need to be simplified or can be more complex, and whether he or she needs to give you additional information or background.

What to Expect the First Time

ORIN AND DABEN *The entry of a high-level guide is almost always gentle, except in some rare cases when the vibration of the guide is dramatically different from yours. In our experiences and in those of the many people we have observed, guides would rather come to you so gently that you would doubt their presence than take the chance of worrying or frightening you. Because most guides enter gently, and most often your trance is light and your own consciousness is present, you may find yourself wondering: Is this my imagination?*

*Guides enter your aura so gently
you may at first doubt their presence.*

Some people begin channeling very easily. With a good alignment of energy fields between you and the guide, it is possible to go into trance without a lengthy period of transition or physical discomfort. Some people take longer to get into trance, needing time to quiet their minds, focus their energies, and align themselves with their guides. Some people go through shudders or strong physical sensations as guides come in, but that is rare. These sensations can usually be eliminated as the person opens and learns to handle the larger energy flowing through his or her body. The most common sensations are heat and tingling. These physical sensations are usually present at the moment of your guide's entry, but usually subside as you continue channeling. If you experience any discomfort, ask your guide to help you open up to his or her energy.

As you continue channeling, you will be able to feel the vibratory presence of your guide as different from your own. Guides have a vibration beyond your normal range of perception, and it may take awhile for you to distinguish between yourself and your guide. You may notice subtle changes in your body, in your posture, or in your breathing. You may observe a subtle change in the rhythm, speed, or pattern of your voice. Some people experience these differences right away, and some don't.

Your guide will deepen the connection as he becomes aware of your ability to handle his energy. You may find yourself receiving suggestions as to how you can increase the strength of your connection. Every time you channel, there is a deeper and stronger link to your guide. To enhance your perception of your guide, you may want to imagine that you are surrounded by a powerful and loving being who is totally accepting of you, protecting, caring, supportive, and wise. Keep pretending that your guide is there, and eventually you will be able to sense your guide as more than your imagination.

You may sense the presence of your guide, but not see a definite form. Some people see lights and colors, and some feel as if they are floating in space. The world of the guides is so full of light that sometimes upon entering it people feel blinded. It is like walking from a dark room into bright sunlight; your eyes need to adjust before you see clearly. When they first reach this higher realm, people sometimes get so overwhelmed by all the sensations that they are unable to bring through concrete messages and advice. They perceive a world of higher vibration, and it may take a while before they can navigate in it.

Reaching your guide requires the ability to focus and concentrate.

If your mind wanders you may lose the connection. Until your mind can easily hold the required level of focus, you may need to use your will to keep the connection firm and solid, keeping your attention on what your guide is talking about. In doing so you may need to let go of any intruding thoughts of your own. Some people have described this as a state of intense inner listening. As you gain skill, you will be able to experience your thoughts and your guide's messages simultaneously. At first the information may look fuzzy. It may seem as if it is "right on the tip of your tongue," or just beyond your grasp. Just go on to the next idea, and you may find that the initial idea becomes clearer as you speak of other things.

When the first words come, you may need to speak them before the next words will flow. This often feels like you are taking a risk because when you normally speak you know beforehand what you are going to say. When you first begin channeling, simply let the information flow. You may be afraid of appearing ridiculous, or think you are bringing in meaningless messages. Let go, trust, and play like a child; be willing to experiment. If the transmission is coming too quickly or too slowly, ask your guide to adjust the pace. At times you may find yourself so inundated with information that it is difficult to express it all. If you are seeing bits and pieces of what seem to be unrelated details, pick an area that interests you and start there.

In the beginning, it is not always obvious from the information transmitted that the guide is high-level. With a high-level guide, there will be a good, positive, uplifting feeling, however. Guides stimulate certain parts of your brain, and at first they may not be skilled at working with you. The connection may take some time to form. Your first words may not accurately reflect the impressions being sent by your guide. During this time, as in any learning process, many doubts may come up. This is not unusual.

Channeling is accompanied by heightened awareness and feelings of well-being.

There is an initial period of experimentation and trial-and-error as your guide explores how to transmit through you with the greatest clarity. There are hundreds of ways to impress our messages upon your consciousness, and we choose the path of least resistance. The more comfortable and at ease you feel with your guide, the more successful your guide has been in impressing his message upon the right sensory path. If the message and the meaning feel distant to you, that usually means that your guide is not connecting through the most direct pathways.

You and your guide may acquire a similarity of thought and ideas. It will often feel as if you are acting as one with your guide. As you achieve attunement and harmony with your guide, the veil between the realms which separate you becomes thinner, and you will be able to see and understand many new things yourself.

People are able to channel far more easily than they expect.

Most people say: "It is so much easier than I thought it would be" or "I have experienced that feeling before—it's so familiar." Let it be easy. Your greatest challenge will be to let yourself speak and not stop the flow by asking if you are really channeling or just making it up.

You may find yourself surprised by the wisdom of what comes through. When you are speaking, you will be overshadowed by the presence of the higher vibration. Do not look for hidden, disguised, obscure, vague, or cryptic messages. You are not searching for buried information. Speak what you may see as obvious, as sometimes the obvious is the most important thing to say. While you are in the space of a higher being, truth will be obvious and often simple.

Be aware that when you start to channel, a verbal message may not always come through. Your guide may simply work with you at an energy level, expanding, opening, and preparing you for the next stage of your development. Or, you may receive guidance as an inner message or mental picture.

At some point after you have begun to channel, experiment. Before calling in your guide, ask a question, and record the answer that comes to your mind. Then call in your guide, and ask the same question. You will almost always find a different answer, a more loving and expansive way of looking at the issue. Even if you and your guide have the same response, you will probably find a slightly different slant to the guide's version.

It is particularly important in the beginning stages to record everything that is spoken. There are several reasons for this. It will help you understand the stages of your progress. It will enable you to look back and see the wisdom of what you brought through. One woman who wasn't sure she was really channeling had her guide's information typed up. She found the notes three months later, and was transfixed as she read them, struck by the wisdom of the information. Things her guide told her she would be experiencing, she had indeed experienced. Reading the transcript helped her believe in the value of what she was doing.

There is another reason for recording what you channel. Once the words are recorded or written, they become part of your reality. They will assist you in creating even higher wisdom in the physical world. Every time you put your words onto tape or paper, you are taking a step toward manifesting them, bringing them closer to physical reality.

Your guide is always present when you call.

People ask, "Why is my guide always present when I call?" Let us explain that we exist in a world beyond time and space, and when we commit to work with you, we are aware of the whole range of our work together. If you change your mind, that changes the picture, but from moment to moment we have a whole picture of our work with you. We experience no time between our sessions with you. To us, there is no stop or start, but only a continuous thread consisting of our time together. When you go into trance, a part of us is once again in your universe; that part of us does not know linear time and is still aware of our last time together. We often experience this as you might experience a telephone line when the connection fades in and out. We simply wait for the next strong connection. We are of a much vaster consciousness than you. We can handle thousands of things at once. Our connection to you takes up a very small portion of our overall awareness, and part of our commitment to you is to maintain a steady clear channel whenever you call.

Your Soul or a Guide?

ORIN AND DABEN *People usually seek explanations about the process when they first begin to channel. They wonder if they are reaching a part of themselves or if the wisdom they are receiving is coming from a guide. Some people, when they channel, experience their guides as separate entities. Others feel they are contacting their higher selves or souls. Let us examine these perceptions.*

You may wonder what it feels like to channel your soul instead of a guide. Many of you are not aware of what your own soul feels like, so it is hard for you to tell the difference between your "soul's" thoughts and the thought-impulses of a "guide." We will refer to your soul as the greater part of you that exists outside of this dimension, lives on after you die, remembers all your lifetimes, chooses your next lifetime and growth opportunities, and so on. We have used the words "soul," "source self," and "higher self" interchangeably.

Unless you are aware of very subtle differences, it may be difficult at an experiential level for you to determine whether you are channeling a guide or bringing through the light of your soul. You can become more aware of the distinction with time and practice.

All channeling is done through your soul.

There must be agreement from your soul before we can talk through you. We broadcast first to your soul. Then your soul sends the message to your mind. Whether or not you are conscious when you channel, we still broadcast to your soul. That is why, even if you are unconscious, the communication will still bear some of the imprint of your soul. Because the message comes through your soul, there will most likely be a sense that the message feels familiar to you.

If you are looking for proof that you are channeling a guide rather than your higher self, you may not find it. What constitutes proof is different for each person. You may bring through information you feel you might not have known on your own, and you may be surprisingly accurate in your visions and predictions. This might be proof to you but not to someone else.

You will come to your own knowingness about this. Some people will claim that it is their higher wisdom, their soul, or their higher self that is speaking. Others will feel with certainty that it is a guide. If you get a guide's name and if you feel it is a guide speaking through you, trust your own deeper knowing.

There may be a feeling that your soul is speaking, not a guide. Sometimes it is your soul speaking. It is fine to channel your higher self or source self, for you are a beautiful and wise being yourself. Your soul's wisdom is far greater than you allow yourself to know. The wisdom from the higher levels of your source self can be as profound as any from a high-level guide.

DUANE When I observe people channeling, I see a real difference in their energy fields as they shift out of what they call their "intuitive" selves—which I see as a harmonizing and smoothing of their energies—and into the guides' space, pulling information and a boost of energy from somewhere outside of themselves. When I talk to people and point out to them when I see the shift, they can almost always identify a change at the same time in their physical sensations, in their thoughts, or in the messages they are receiving.

Getting Your Guide's Name

SANAYA AND DUANE Some people get their guide's name right away. Some get sounds and letters, which later form into a name. Some people say that they try so hard to get the name "right" that they became confused. Only later when they relax do they get the name. Others get a name weeks after they ask for it, and some people never do get a name. Guides have told us that they aren't as concerned about the "right" name as they are about wanting people to feel good about the name. Many people found that the name changed or altered slightly over the first few days as they channeled, until they had a name that felt good and seemed to fit.

Guides say that getting your guide's name directly from your guide, rather than being told the name by another guide, strengthens your connection. Orin also tells people: "Do not attach too much importance to having your guide's name in the beginning. In our realm we know each other by energy patterns, and we seek a name that most fits with our energy, including names we had in other lifetimes."

Some people found that by getting the first letter or a sound of the name, they could work with it on their own until they found the right combination of sounds or letters. Sometimes as they read something they saw a name and knew it was their guide's. Some people had several names and several guides. One woman had twelve guides who called themselves the "Council of Twelve."

Another woman had three guides, who called themselves "Dear Ones." One guide would answer most of the questions, but occasionally, depending upon the question, another guide would respond. One man constantly asked his guide for a name, but his guide kept telling him "we are of the no name." Another woman who has a very informative and wise guide never has received a name. After two years she finally stopped asking for one. Let whatever experience you have be the right one.

Many people have looked up the meaning of their guides' names and found that it had special significance for them. A woman who works with flower essences felt/heard the energy of her guide and the name "Maya." Looking up the name later, she discovered that it meant "the gathering of flowers." One man kept dreaming about moons the night he began to channel. The name his guide had given him was Margaret and when he looked up the name he found it was derived from the Greek word meaning "pearl," which came from the Persian word meaning "moon." Play with the name, and let it evolve.

If you feel ready to learn to channel, go on to Chapter 6. If you would like to read about our and other's experiences with channeling, go to Chapter 10.

SECTION II
OPENING TO CHANNEL

6 ACHIEVING A TRANCE STATE

Guide to Using Exercises

SANAYA AND DUANE If you want to connect with a high-level guide and learn to channel, the exercises and processes that follow will help you to do so. They are based on the processes Orin and DaBen gave us for the Opening to Channel course. Several hundred people have used these processes to effectively open to channel. For this book Orin and DaBen have included additional information to make it possible for you as a reader to learn to channel without our direct assistance or the setting of the course. Orin and DaBen will provide you with guidance and energy assistance for your opening if you ask for it, and your own guide will help you as well.

It is best to use these exercises and processes in a sequential manner. Proceed through them at your own speed, and start at the skill level you are at now. We have included them in one place so you can start from the beginning and go all the way through them in one afternoon if you are ready. Alternatively, you may want to do them over a period of weeks. As you open to channel, be loving and patient with yourself and allow play to direct some of your efforts. Keep in mind that you are unique and your experience will be your own.

As with any new skill, some readiness and willingness to explore areas that are new for you is important. It is common for people to be excited, even nervous or anxious, when they approach an opportunity such as channeling. Do these exercises and processes only when you feel ready to learn to channel. If you do not feel ready now, you may want to skip this section and go directly to Section III, Chapter 10, to read about our and other people's channeling experiences. If you desire to channel, that time will come, probably much sooner than you think.

You can prepare yourself to channel; you may already have done much to get ready. To start you should be able to achieve and maintain a relaxed state, and from this relaxed state be able to hold a focus and concentrate for at least five minutes. You may have achieved this during meditation or self-hypnosis.

If you feel confident about relaxing and focusing, move quickly through the first two exercises and onto the third exercise, Attuning with Life-Force Energy. Remember that relaxation and focus are key elements to channeling, so as you develop as a channel, these will be areas you can work on to easily increase your ability to channel more and more clearly.

If you cannot easily achieve a relaxed and focused trance state, then the first two exercises will assist you. Spend a few days becoming familiar with relaxation techniques and learn to concentrate as shown in the exercise on concentration. One way to condition yourself to the trance state is through guided meditation tapes. You can make these yourself or use those made by others. The steps of the exercises and processes are laid out so that you can use them as a guideline for making your own recording to lead yourself into trance. Orin and DaBen have made tapes to assist you in all of the processes, which you may want to use. (See Appendix for tape programs.)

There are times when it is best not to work with these exercises or learn to channel. When you are ill, temporarily in grief or shock, or going through very disturbing times of crisis, it is better not to learn to channel. Similarly you will not want to learn to channel during extended periods of depression or times when you are exhausted or physically depleted. It is best to make your first connection with a guide when you are feeling rested, healthy, and positive. After you get a clear connection to your guide, you will be able to use the connection to assist you in getting out of negative emotional states. If you have unresolved fears, doubts, or questions, wait to channel until you have examined them thoroughly and found acceptable resolution.

The way to excellence in channeling is the same as for any skill—continued study, determination, the intention to succeed, a heartfelt love for the process, and responsiveness to those things which help you improve. The greatest teacher of all is your desire to become an excellent, clear channel.

The exercises and processes that follow are structured and represent one way you can learn to channel. Each time you use them, reach as high as you can and you will grow in your ability to reach upward and connect with the higher realms. Use these processes when you first open, or create your own processes around them. Once you have learned to channel, and are familiar with the experience, we encourage you to drop the forms and processes you have learned here and develop your own style. We go into trance easily with little or no ritual.

People have asked us, "Do I need to surround myself in white light?" You may want to start by surrounding yourself with an image of a bubble of white light. You are not using the light to protect yourself, but instead to increase your vibration. The only time we use the image of a bubble of light is when we're assisting others, as it seems to help people let go of doubts and stay in a higher state. When Sanaya goes into trance as Orin, she experiences herself as letting go and surrendering to a higher being. She does not surround herself with a bubble of light before Orin comes in, for when Orin comes in he IS light.

It is best to adopt a joyful attitude in any channeling state. Stay with what is joyful. Experiment! Don't let anything become a must or a should. The more you get used to channeling states, the more you will discover the subtleties that exist in these spaces. The spaces you can travel to when you channel are endless. They are doorways into unlimited new experiences of growth.

To practice relaxation techniques, go to the Achieving a Relaxed State exercise. After you are able to relax go to the exercise, Holding a Focus and Concentration. Once you have mastered both, go to the exercise, Attuning with Life-Force Energy.

Exercise from Orin and DaBen

Achieving a Relaxed State

Goal: This exercise is basic preparation for going into trance. We want your experience of channeling to be relaxing, easy, and joyful.

Preparation: Pick a time when you will be undisturbed for at least ten or fifteen minutes. Turn off the phone. If other people live in the house, let them know you want to be left alone and close the door. It is amazing how a peaceful, meditative state can attract children and people who suddenly want to talk to you. Create an enjoyable, soothing environment around you. Wear loose clothes; it is important to feel comfortable. Pick a time when you feel wide awake. If you have just eaten or you are tired, wait until later. Put on some soothing, gentle, calming music. (See suggested music in Appendix.)

Steps:
1. Find a comfortable sitting position, either on a chair or the floor, which you can easily hold for ten or fifteen minutes.
2. Close your eyes and begin breathing calmly and slowly, taking about twenty slow, rhythmic, connected breaths into your upper chest.
3. Let all your concerns go. Imagine them vanishing. Every time a thought comes up, imagine it on a blackboard, then effortlessly erase it, or imagine putting each thought into a bubble that floats away.
4. Relax your body. Feel yourself growing serene, calm, and tranquil. In your imagination, travel through your body, relaxing each part. Mentally relax your feet, legs, thighs, stomach, chest, arms, hands, shoulders, neck, head, and face. Let your jaw be slightly open, and relax the muscles around your eyes.
5. Put up a bubble of white light around you. Imagine its size, shape, and brightness. Play with making it larger and smaller until it feels just right.

6. When you are calm and relaxed and ready to return, bring your attention slowly back into the room. Savor and enjoy your state of calm and peace.

Evaluation: If you feel more calm and relaxed than normal, not how you imagine others to feel, but for you, then proceed to the next exercise, Holding a Focus and Concentration.

If you do not feel more calm and relaxed than normal, either stop for now and do this exercise again at another time, or go back over the steps and spend more time relaxing each part of your body. Try inventing your own processes or thoughts that will bring you to a more relaxed and calm state. If you are not successful at relaxing, usually it is sufficient to practice every day for twenty minutes or so for one to two weeks to grow accustomed to deeper relaxation and inner stillness. This regime is not absolutely essential, but helps you become accustomed to the state of mind that is best for a guide's entry.

Focus—An Element of the Channeling Space

ORIN AND DABEN *An important aspect of channeling is being able to focus, so you can receive and put out energy at the same time. If you are healing someone, you want to act as a channel, receiving the higher energy at the same time you perform whatever functions are required. If you are channeling verbal information with your guide, you will want to receive information from your guide at the same time you speak. The challenge in channeling for some people is that they receive easily, but find it difficult to speak at the same time. This kind of mental-physical dexterity can be learned.*

When people sit to meditate or relax, everything on their minds may begin to surface. One woman said that every time she sat down to channel, she would think of everything she had to do. She would think of people she had forgotten to call, letters that needed answering, and all the things around the house that needed fixing. She decided to keep a pad of paper to jot down these thoughts as they came up. Once she knew they were recorded, she could relax and go into a deeper trance. She said that if she didn't write them down, she would get so concerned about the possibility of forgetting them that she would have difficulty going any further and would eventually stop. This worked for her. If you have the same problem, see if it works for you.

Spending time getting used to expanded states of consciousness is important. Learn to quiet the normal flow of your thoughts and concentrate on one idea at a time. Don't worry if you find it hard to focus now, for as you continue, it will get easier. Your ability to concentrate and achieve one-pointed attention upward is what allows a clear connection with your guide.

Exercise from Orin and DaBen

Holding a Focus and Concentration

Goal: The mind is naturally fast and active. For channeling, the mind needs to develop some degree of skill in directing this speed and activity into concentrating on the flow of information coming from your guide.

Preparation: Be able to achieve a relaxed state, physically and emotionally. If you like, listen to some very soothing, calming music. If you want, keep pen and paper nearby.

Steps:
1. When you feel relaxed, pick one *positive* quality you would like to bring into your life. It might be something such as love, compassion, joy, or peace.
2. As you think of that quality, imagine how many ways you could experience it in your life. How would feeling that way change your life? What would you do differently if you had more of that quality? How would having it change your relationships to other people?
3. Hold the images and thoughts clearly in your mind for as long as you can. Try this for at least five minutes.
4. Watch the intruding thoughts that come up about unrelated topics. If they are important and you need to remember them, jot them down so you can let them go from your mind.

At other times repeat the exercise, focusing on an object such as a flower, crystal, or any object you feel an affinity to. This time observe the object—noting its color, size, and detail—for at least five minutes without intruding thoughts.

You might also try imagining a great being, a master, sitting in front of you. Imagine you are looking into the eyes of the master and aligning with his or her higher vibration. See if you can hold this image and connection for at least five minutes.

Evaluation: Notice how long you are able to hold a focus. Five minutes is a very good start. If you cannot hold this focus for at least five minutes, start with a minute every day for a week or so, until you can stay focused for at least five minutes at a time. When you can hold a focus for five minutes or longer, go on to the next exercise, Attuning with Life-Force Energy.

Exercise from Orin and DaBen
Attuning with Life-Force Energy

Goal: When channeling, you need to sense the presence of your guide at a feeling, intuitive level. Sensing the subtle vibrations of life-force energy begins to open your awareness.

Preparation: Be able to relax, and have mastered concentrating for at least five minutes, as in the Holding a Focus and Concentration exercise. Prepare yourself in the same way as for the Achieving a Relaxed State exercise, including the use of music. Find a time which will be uninterrupted and a place where you will be undisturbed. Have crystals and flowers within easy reach. (*Needed:* Two crystals, preferably real quartz and amethyst, one of each. Two flowers or plants, of any kind that you may touch.)

Steps:
1. Find a comfortable position, relax your body, quiet your thoughts, calm your emotions. Let yourself have at least two to three minutes to relax. Imagine calling all of your energy back to yourself from everywhere in the universe. Imagine letting go of anyone else's energy that you have taken on and sending it upwards.
2. Take one of the crystals in your right hand. Send out your welcome to the crystal. Feel its perfect pattern. Imagine that each crystal has a special type of energy that can amplify something good for you. Really sense the energy in this crystal. Mentally ask the crystal about its purpose. See if you can put words to what you are sensing. Give the crystal at least two or three minutes of your attention.
3. Put that crystal down and pick up the other crystal. Do the same thing with this crystal and notice any differences you sense between the crystals. It may feel as if the energy is coming from your imagination. That is as it should be. Notice that you CAN sense energy at this subtle level.
4. Put the crystals away and pick up one of the flowers or touch one of the plants. Greet this flower or plant and get to know it.

Notice how you are able to feel its aliveness, its energy. Spend at least two or three minutes sensing and greeting it.

5. Put it down, and pick up the other flower or touch the other plant. Greet this flower or plant and get to know it. Notice how you are able to feel its aliveness, its energy. Notice the differences in energy between the two flowers or plants.

6. Come fully out of trance, stretch your body, open your eyes.

7. As you recall your insights, fill yourself with the conviction that you are easily able to sense the subtle energies of other life forms. Recall as many of the qualities and differences in the life-force of the crystals and flowers as you can.

Evaluation: If you are able to sense these subtle vibrations, even slightly, even if it feels like you are just making it up, that is good. Proceed to the next exercise, Trance Posture and Position. If you can't sense anything, repeat this exercise at other times until you can.

Exercise from Orin and DaBen
Trance Posture and Position

Goal: To find the posture and position that helps to best support your trance and allows you to reach and harmonize with higher spiritual levels.

Preparation: Have completed the Attuning with Life-Force Energy exercise, and have a basic ability to relax and hold a focus. Wear loose clothing and sit in a comfortable upright sitting position, either on the floor or in a chair. Sit straight, and stack your vertebrae one on top of another, in a position you can hold for twenty minutes or so. If you are on the floor, you may want the support of a pillow under your buttocks. It is best when your physical body is at a certain level of comfort, not necessarily pain-free, but so that any pain or discomfort does not distract you. Your environment should not be too warm or too cold. Put on some music that will help lift you to a high spiritual feeling.

Steps:
1. Close your eyes and begin to relax your body, calm your emotions, and quiet your mind. Spend at least two or three minutes relaxing and quieting your thoughts. Call any energy you have scattered out in the universe back to yourself.
2. Imagine that you are going to take a journey upwards into the higher realms of light and love. Adjust your energy so that you begin to feel yourself in a high spiritual space. Use whatever images help you evoke that special feeling. Imagine a moment under the stars, or remember the feeling of reverence you have in a church or temple. Connect with whatever takes you into a higher space and allows you to feel more at one with the God-within.
3. Go with the flow of that mood. You may want to adjust your position. Experiment with *slight* movements of your face, neck, and shoulders. Discover which positions allow you to feel more expansive and think in higher ways. Take a deep breath into your upper chest. Notice how your posture shifts and how your head

comes into a different position. Let your head feel as though it is floating. It can be tilted slightly forward or back, right or left. Play with the angle of your head. Let your thoughts slow down. Let your stomach relax. Notice how some of the smallest movements in posture or position produce large changes in how you feel.

4. Experience your inner senses. Listen through all of your senses. Notice that some of your internal chatter and busyness is going away. Notice also that you are more aware of your surroundings, of the room, the sounds, smells, and energies. Let that awareness boost you higher.

5. Notice your breathing. Let your hands and your wrists relax. You may even tingle a bit and grow warmer as you begin to open the channel to a higher energy. Let yourself open to the higher realms beyond the earth plane. Imagine all the cells in your right-brain, your receiving mind, reflecting perfectly the higher planes of reality, much like mirrors. Imagine the higher energy flowing from your right-brain into your left-brain, your conscious mind, with perfect precision and clarity. Observe your mind as if it were a clear mountain lake reflecting the higher realms. Spend a few minutes absorbing this higher vibration.

6. Go as high as you can with your mind. You may feel a sense of love and compassion that is greater than usual. Let yourself feel centered, balanced, loving, and open. Experiment with coming in and out of this space. Notice how your body follows the change. Note how you can influence this feeling directly and spontaneously with your thoughts.

7. When you have explored some of what is possible from this space, come back into the room, fully present and alert.

Practice being in this channeling space in varying circumstances and places. Learn to identify those times during the day when you might be in a spontaneous channeling space: concentrating on the solution to a problem; pouring out love to someone, perhaps helping them with advice; painting, drawing, teaching, etc. Do not let any particular posture or set of circumstances become a ritual or necessity. Learn to establish a good link or channeling state under all kinds of circumstances.

Evaluation: If you were able to get a greater than normal sense of love and compassion or an expansive feeling from this exercise, proceed to Chapter 7, Opening to Channel. If you found it particularly difficult, you may be making it more complicated than it is. Relax, let go of your thoughts about what it should feel like, and work with this exercise again—at your own pace.

7 CONNECTING WITH YOUR GUIDE

Greetings and Welcome

ORIN AND DABEN *This is it! The time to Open to Channel is now. You've dreamed of it, read about it, thought about it, and now you will do it!*

In the first process, you will be welcomed by the guides, call for your special guide, and carry on a "mental" conversation with him or her. You will be able to determine if this is the guide you will verbally channel; if it is you will proceed to the next process, Verbally Channeling Your Guide.

If it's been a while since you read the beginning of the book, we suggest you reread Chapters 3, 4, and 5 about who the guides are, how it will feel to channel and how the guides communicate with you.

Only do these processes if you feel ready, are in good health, feeling positive emotionally, and feel that you have resolved most of your questions about how to recognize a high guide. Don't forget—you're not alone in this endeavor—in fact one of the reasons channeling may be easier than you expect is because you're going to have help from your guide.

Process from Orin and DaBen

Ceremony of Welcome to the Guide's Realm and First Meeting with Your Guide

Goal: This is to welcome you to the guide's realm and to enable you to gain a conscious impression of the guide you will be channeling.

Preparation: Have completed Attuning with Life-Force Energy and Trance Posture and Position exercises in Chapter 6 before doing this process. Put on some soothing, beautiful music that gives you a feeling of reverence and uplifts you; select music that has previously assisted you in feeling expanded, as in the Trance Posture and Position exercise.

Steps:

1. Get into your trance posture; make sure it is a comfortable position with your back erect. Once again examine your body position, starting with your feet. Notice the placement of your hands, back, and legs. Become aware of your breathing. Close your eyes, and begin to take a few deep breaths. Enter into the trance state you have practiced.

2. Imagine yourself going higher and higher, transcending ordinary reality and entering into a higher dimension of love, light, and joy. Imagine yourself being bathed in light; feel the space about you full of beautiful, soft, white light.

3. Imagine that many beings of light are coming closer to join you. Feel their love and caring for you. Open your heart to receive them. Imagine the doorways opening between your reality and theirs. Sense the presence of many loving and high beings all around you, welcoming you into the higher realms, where there is joy and unconditional love. Imagine them creating a doorway for you.

4. Realize it is no coincidence that you are making this connection. See the whole chain of events that led you to this moment, the chance meetings, the books, and the changes that have already been occurring in your life. Your guide and the guides are aware

of you and hold a special welcome for you as you join more closely with them.

5. Imagine that there is a doorway in front of you. On the other
side of this doorway is a world of light, of higher vibration, and
of accelerated growth for you. Go inward, into your heart, and ask
yourself if you are ready to make a larger commitment to yourself
and to your path of service. When you are ready, *walk through this
doorway.* (If you are not ready now, it will be all right if you choose
to walk through the door even weeks later.) Feel the light pouring
upon you, healing and cleansing you. Accept this new level of light
into your life. Be aware that this is a very real doorway and that
your life will begin to change after you walk through it.

6. There is a plan for mankind's evolution being broadcast by many
high beings. Sit silently, and imagine you are tuning into this broadcast. Pretend that your energies are aligning with this plan, so that
as your path unfolds from this day everything you do will be in
accordance with the greater plan. You will be a channel for light
in whatever way you choose to pursue your growth.

7. Continue to adjust your posture as you go higher and higher.
Ask for the highest guide and teacher who is aligned with you to
come forward. Imagine that your guide, a special guide, is coming
forward. Sense this guide, feel his or her love for you. Be open to
receive. Feel your heart welcoming this guide. Feel the response.
Believe that it is really happening! Your imagination is the closest
ability you have to channeling, and it is the easiest connection your
guide has to you at first.

8. What does your guide look or feel like? Let impressions come
in. Do not censor or judge the sensations, images, impressions, or
information you are getting. Become familiar with this high feeling
of your guide.

9. Greet your guide in your mind. Ask your guide if he or she is
from the light. Affirm that you are asking for the highest possible
guide who is aligned with your higher good and your spiritual path.
You may want to mentally carry on a conversation with this guide
until you feel comfortable about allowing the guide to come closer.
If you do not feel good about this guide, ask whether he or she
has anything of value to impart to you, and then ask him or her

to leave. Ask again for a high, healing master teacher to come to you. (If you have questions at this point, refer again to Chapter 4.) When you feel good about a guide, go to the next step.

10. Ask your guide to begin doing all that he or she can to open the channel, now that you are committed and ready to verbally channel. Ask your guide to send a mental message if there is anything further that you need to do to prepare to verbally channel.

11. When you have these messages, thank all the beings of light, and feel their appreciation for you. Thank your guide, and ask him or her to help you get ready to verbally channel. Say goodbye, and come back slowly and easily to your normal reality. You have now made a connection with the guide you will verbally channel.

Evaluation: If you were able to walk through the doorway, and if you were able to mentally sense and meet your guide, proceed to the next process, Verbally Channeling Your Guide.

If you were able to walk through the doorway but not able to sense or mentally talk to a guide, repeat this process at another time. Do not proceed to the next process until you have mentally met and conversed with your guide.

If you did not feel ready to walk through the doorway, do not proceed to the next process. Walking through this doorway and making a larger commitment to yourself are big steps. Before proceeding, you may want to read about Sanaya's, Duane's, and other people's experiences with channeling in Chapters 10 through 13. When you do decide to go through the doorway, go back and repeat this process until you establish a good mental connection to your guide.

SANAYA When Orin first offered me the opportunity to walk through the doorway, I took three weeks to say "yes." I thought about it intently beforehand. Within days after "mentally" walking through this doorway, my life began to change dramatically. Opportunities to serve and help others began coming from everywhere. Duane's experience was almost identical. He, too, took time to think things over before making the commitment. He, too, experienced dramatic changes within days.

Process from Orin and DaBen
Verbally Channeling Your Guide

Goal: This process is to bring your guide in through your voice, get your guide's name, and answer questions in trance.

Preparation: Have completed all prior exercises and processes. Read through this entire process before you begin, so that you are familiar with its overall direction. Whenever you verbally channel, use a tape recorder. You will gain invaluable insights from listening again to your channeling. Notice where the microphone is on your recorder, so you don't hold it away from you or cover it up, or else use a separate microphone. Label the tape with the date, side, and perhaps the topic you're channeling on, and put it in the tape recorder. Test the recorder and the microphones, and feel your voice connecting with them. These are your transmitting devices. They assist you in recording your channeling and saving it for future use. Put light around your recorder and microphones, and visualize them receiving your channeling. When you are in a trance state you may find that mechanical things can give you difficulties. Remember to turn on the tape recorder and push the right buttons.

Be sure you have read the earlier sections about a guide's first entry and getting your guide's name. Have the Questions to Ask Your Guide ready, including the Personal Questions. You may want to record these questions and have them ready to play back on a separate tape recorder. If you are with a friend, give them the questions to ask you, and be sure they have read the Instructions for Assisting and Guiding a Partner Through First Meeting.

We suggest that you remain in trance no longer than about forty minutes the first time. There is no danger with longer periods, but they may be tiring. If at any time you find the connection growing weaker or feel yourself becoming tired, come fully out of trance. You have made the first connection, there will be many more. Wait an hour or so before going into trance again.

Steps:
1. If you wish, put on some special music that will assist you, and find a comfortable erect sitting position. Close your eyes and

go into your trance position and enter your trance state. Breath deeply and slowly into your upper chest. Imagine a golden light coming into a place in the back of your head and upper neck to activate the connection. If you want, surround yourself with the image of a bubble of white light.

2. Now, imagine energy and light flowing into your throat and vocal cords. Open these areas to the high, light energy of your guide. One way to open these areas is to say the word "om" with each exhale. Relax even more and repeat the sound for several minutes. Let the sound and vibration lift you.

3. Believe that you can make this connection with ease. Adjust your energy so that you feel yourself connecting with the higher realms of light and love. Imagine that you are again going upwards, expanding your being, and that the guides are once again creating a doorway for you to walk through.

4. Call to you the same guide you met earlier. Greet him or her again. You may want to talk to this guide in your mind once more. Make sure this guide feels high, loving, and wise to you. When you feel confident and ready, proceed to let your guide come into your aura and energy more closely.

5. Now imagine that you are inviting your guide more fully into your energy systems. Imagine that your guide is gently penetrating your aura, and, softly and lovingly, coming closer to you. Feel the presence of your guide growing stronger. Keep bringing the connection closer. Ask your guide to assist you. You may want to continue to make the slightest changes in your posture, in your head and neck position to intensify the connection and keep the energy in the back of your head and neck open. Imagine that your guide is joining with you, so that you are sitting in his or her light, but also know that your personal energy is inviolate. Imagine your sense of self as strong and your feeling of "self" intact.

6. Now let your guide come fully into your aura. Your guide's vibration is very light, loving, and wise, and you will most probably feel a loving presence overshadowing you. Your guide may feel as if he or she is amplifying the best in you. There should be a sense of well-being. Continue to open only if the guide feels high and affirms he or she is from the light. If there is a sense of heaviness, resistance, or negativity, do not continue to bring in this guide. Ask for a higher guide, and demand that this guide leave.

7. Notice your emotions. There is often a sense of compassion as we join with you, for we are beings of love. You may feel a sense of calmness and tranquility. We know it takes practice and time to strengthen the connection. You may call upon our energy, Orin and DaBen, to help with your opening. We applaud you for your willingness today to make this initial link.

8. Now imagine the connection growing even stronger. If your mind is saying, "I wonder if it is just me" or asking, "Have I really connected with a guide?" let that thought go, and for now believe that you have indeed connected with a high-level guide, even if you cannot sense or prove the reality of it.

9. Turn your tape recorder on. Ask your guide for a name or sound by which you may know him or her. Give yourself plenty of time. If you do not receive a name, ask for the first letter or sound. Be sure to record the name. You may find you and your guide changing the name over the next several weeks. Some people find that there is more than one guide present; they may get several names. If you get a name move on to the next step. It is all right though if you don't get a name at first—or ever—for not all guides choose to take names. If you aren't getting a name after a short while, move on to the next step.

10. Start channeling by asking your guide questions. Pick questions from the Questions to Ask Your Guide When You First Start Channeling. If you are having difficulty receiving answers to the Questions of Universal Nature, ask your guide Questions of Personal Concern. If you don't get specific answers, see if you are getting pictures or symbols, then speak these. If you aren't receiving answers to the questions and don't get any images, ask your guide to further open and strengthen the connection. Then, to get your verbal connection started, describe any physical sensations or whatever you are feeling out loud. Record your answers. If you find it difficult to speak directly, as if you are the guide, relay the messages second hand, such as "my guide says ... "

to start. If you feel any discomfort, ask your guide to help you open the area in pain.

11. After you and your guide have established the ability to answer questions, continue to answer questions for as long as you feel comfortable. When you or your guide is finished, before you close, sit quietly enjoying your guide's energy. No talking is necessary. Find the harmony that this state brings.

12. When you are ready, ask your guide to strengthen the connection so that it will be even easier to connect the next time you channel.

13. After you have finished, thank your guide, and feel his or her gratitude for you. Come fully out of trance. Stretch your body, move around, open your eyes, and bring yourself to full, alert, and aware consciousness.

Evaluation: Congratulations on Opening to Channel, you have begun a very special relationship. Welcome to the joy and adventure that lie ahead. Please read and join in the Graduation Ceremony, which is the last section in this chapter.

If you haven't reached your guide, do this exercise again until you do. Concentration, patience, and persistence are usually required as you develop the ability to raise yourself to the proper vibratory key. Keep asking your guide to help you with the connection, and find quiet time alone for your guide to reach you. If you tried this process by yourself the first time, you may want to arrange to have a friend assist you the next time by asking questions and being a listener for your guide's answers. See the Instructions for Assisting and Guiding a Partner Through First Meeting.)

If after some attempts you have not made the connection, you may want to use another method, such as calling in your guide and letting the ideas flow through your mind into your hands at a computer, typewriter, or with pen and paper. Occasionally people find it easier to get their first channeling connection in this way.

If you feel spacey coming out of trance, you haven't fully broken the connection. Instruct yourself to come fully out of trance, perhaps stretching your body and moving around. If you still feel spacey, go outside or walk around indoors. Do something that requires left-brain, analytical thinking.

We have instructed you to channel with your eyes closed as it is easier to focus and receive inner messages when visual stimulus is removed. Most people prefer to continue to channel with their eyes closed; however, it is possible, and perfectly acceptable, to channel with your eyes open.

Questions to Ask Your Guide When You First Start Channeling

SANAYA AND DUANE   If you are not doing these processes with a friend, you might want to record the following questions on a second tape recorder with long pauses in between. As you connect with your guide, turn on the second tape recorder as well so you can answer these questions in trance. If you have a friend assisting you, have him or her ask your guide these questions. If your guide answers in very short replies, ask for elaborations on the answer. The purpose of the questions is to establish and stabilize a verbal connection to your guide.

Some people find it easier to receive answers to the Questions of Universal Nature when they first start channeling, but others do not. If you are having difficulty receiving answers to Questions of Universal Nature, ask the Questions of Personal Concern that follow. If you don't get specific answers but instead see symbols and images with your inner eyes, speak about these images.

Questions from Orin and DaBen
Questions of Universal Nature

1. Is it possible to live with real joy? What is real joy? How might people distinguish true joy from the illusion of joy? Is there a difference between the joy of the higher self and the joy of the personality? Is it possible to have both?

2. Is the higher self different from the self that people know? How might people reach their higher selves? Is it the same for each person? What does the higher self feel like?

3. What is the function of the will? Can it be directed without force? How might one direct it in other ways to get what one wants? How can your will serve you? What things can you do to create what you want (processes, techniques, etc.)?

4. How might people bring more light into their lives?

5. Does everyone have a life-purpose? What are some of the reasons people choose to be born? What kinds of things are people working on in earth lifetimes?

6. Is this truly an abundant and friendly universe?

7. Is it possible to be affected by other people's thoughts or emotions? How might people recognize that they have been affected by others, and what might they do about it?

8. Does every relationship have a purpose? Is everything you see in another person a reflection of what you are working on in yourself? Is it true that by changing yourself you can change the relationship?

9. Is the future preordained? Is there free will? What do people gain by having free will? How might people create the futures they want?

10. Does the earth itself have a consciousness or life-force? What is its nature? What does the earth want right now; is she sending out any messages?

11. What can be done now by an individual to contribute to world peace? What can be done by an individual to contribute to the conservation of nature?

12. What is the purpose of learning to channel? How will it serve me and mankind?

Questions from Orin and DaBen
Questions of Personal Concern

Some people find these questions elicit answers more easily than the Questions of Universal Nature. Ask your guide several of these questions. If you don't get any response and are not doing the process with a friend, describe into your tape recorder what you are feeling, including thoughts, physical sensations, etc. It is important to start talking, even if it just feels like you, rather than your guide, in the beginning. When you have a verbal connection with your guide, go back to Questions of Universal Concern.

General Questions
1. What is my life purpose?
2. What are my lessons in this lifetime?
3. How can I create more abundance in my life?
4. What am I learning in my relationship with_____?
5. What is my highest path right now?
6. How can I best express my creativity?
7. How can I achieve inner peace? What will my inner peace feel like?

Personal Questions
Add questions you would like your guide to answer:
1.

2.

3.

4.

5.

Instructions for Assisting and Guiding a Partner Through First Meeting

If you are assisting someone in opening to channel, read these instructions carefully. This is a special time for the channel and can be for you as well. As a partner, you can be of enormous assistance to the channel as he opens up to his guide for the first time. You can read the process to your partner and help when he first goes into trance and connects with his guide. You can help with the tape recorder, making sure it is on and ready to record the guide's answers to questions.

Have your partner go into trance, following instructions 1 through 8 in the Verbally Channeling Your Guide process. After he has achieved a trance state and called in his guide, turn on the tape recorder and ask the guide's name. If a name is received, ask how it is spelled, and write it down. If a name is not received, ask your partner if there is a letter or a sound. If he continues to get no response, ask the guide if he or she is ready to answer questions. From now on it will help to talk directly to the guide, and use the guide's name, if the guide has given a name. If the guide agrees, first ask Questions of Universal Nature. If the channel has difficulty receiving answers to this type of question, move to Questions of Personal Concern. If your partner still has trouble establishing a voice connection, slowly ask some of the Questions on Physical Sensations. Getting the channel to start talking in trance is the most important thing you can do right now.

The purpose of these questions is to get the channel to open his throat center and speak. Do not worry if there is no immediate response. Remember, some people will hesitate for a long time before answering; give the channel plenty of time. Silence often means he is accessing his guide, so give him enough time to "find" the answers. If the channel answers the questions with very short and quick replies, encourage him to answer in greater detail—perhaps by asking questions about some part of the answer; take an interest in the information.

If the channel has established a verbal connection but is still having difficulty receiving answers, ask questions about someone the channel doesn't know, a friend you know well enough to be able to later give meaningful feedback about the answers. Give the guide your friend's name, and then ask questions such as "How can I help this person?" or "What am I learning in my relationship with him or her?" Do not ask for predictions or questions that involve detailed answers, such as dates or times.

It is best for your partner to be in trance no more than about twenty to forty minutes total. When he comes out of trance, your positive feedback and enthusiasm will help to solidify the connection. If your partner has not established a verbal link with his guide, be supportive and do this process again at another time.

Questions from Orin and DaBen

Questions for Partner on Physical Sensations

Ask these questions only if your partner isn't able to bring through verbal answers to Questions to Ask Your Guide. As soon as your partner is speaking easily, go back to the Questions of Universal Nature.

1. Do you have any physical sensations?
How does your body feel?
2. What are your emotions right now?
3. Do you see or hear anything?
4. Describe what you are experiencing as best as you can.

If the channel isn't feeling anything or is having difficulty answering these questions, ask the guide if he or she could strengthen the connection. If your partner says he feels blocked, ask the guide to show him what to do. Your positive, helpful attitude is most important in helping the guide come through your partner. Your encouragement, interest, patience, and love are the most important qualities you can offer.

Graduation Ceremony— Congratulations on Opening to Channel

ORIN AND DABEN   *When a guide has been consciously received, there is much joy in our plane. Our excitement at this opening is immense, and we celebrate when we reach through with our light to earth. Not only does your guide rejoice at making the conscious connection, we all celebrate your ability to communicate with us. We celebrate with love. Your expanded consciousness into our realms is similar to a new life being born. It is your birth into light.*

> *We celebrate when you establish a connection with us.*

Now that you have opened to channel, many good changes will occur in your life if you want them. Your desires will be fulfilled far more rapidly than in the past. As you evolve spiritually, it will be increasingly important to be precise about your wants. Think about them carefully, because you will receive them. If you had everything you wanted now, what would you desire next? This question will come up, for many of your goals will come to you. Use positive thoughts and words, and pay attention to how you speak. You will be more connected and linked with the universal mind. You will have access to higher realms of creativity, essence, and light. Your words and thoughts will carry more influence. You will have increasing power to heal or hurt with your words or thoughts. State your needs and desires positively. Focus on what you want, rather than on what you don't want, because you will get what you focus on. Use uplifting words and pay attention to what is good and right in people rather than what they are doing wrong.

> *Welcome to our realms of light.*

Life need not be hard. You no longer need to struggle. We can help you help yourself. Remember to ask, for we can only assist you when you ask for assistance. You will be helped in every area of your life. Your guide will help you acquire all the tools you need to make your life work. You are part of a larger community when you channel, the community of beings that exist in the higher planes of reality. Your harmonious feelings and thoughts greatly contribute to our work together. When you are upset, we feel it. We will work with you to help you calm the turbulence of your life, to help you live in greater ease and peace.

Life can be easy— things can happen joyfully.

Your willingness to be open, to receive, to trust yourself, to experience the world in new ways, and to use this opportunity for growth is all that is needed. There is much ahead for you, for opening to channel is the beginning of a new world. As you are ready, people will come to you to be assisted in their growth. Your integrity and responsibility are of utmost importance. Represent yourself well to the world, be humble, recognize the light in others, and speak well of people. You are the leaders, teachers, and healers of the new age. Because you have brought in more light, you will be magnetic to people. You have walked through a doorway with this opening. You will even more easily make a difference in the world. Your choices will become clearer. You will begin to see the probable futures ahead of you, and be able to consciously choose which path you want to take. Be willing to put your path above all else, and make a greater commitment to yourself. Let go of any obligations to other people's paths unless they are parts of your path.

You will be working with the forces of evolution and swimming with the current rather than against it. Make a commitment to having your life work. Allow your greater good to come to you. You can go all the way to higher consciousness in just one lifetime.

It is possible to achieve higher consciousness in one lifetime now more than ever before. There is much joy and laughter in our realms, so do not take yourself too seriously. Play with the universe, and let the universe play with you. Bringing through your guide is just the beginning of a wonderful journey filled with the mystery of discovery, the joy of learning, and the well-being that comes from living in the light.

SANAYA AND DUANE   We recommend that you take a break, giving yourself a little time to integrate your experiences. After your break, you may wish to go on to Reading for Others, Chapter 8, or read about Duane's and Sanaya's experiences with channeling, as well as other people's openings in Chapters 10 through 13. If you want to read more about developing your channeling, go directly to Chapter 14.

8 READING FOR OTHERS

Giving Readings to Other People

ORIN AND DABEN   *In the course of your channeling, you will most probably be presented with the opportunity to channel for other people. It is a special occasion for people when they have the opportunity to meet your guide. You will enjoy your channeling most when you channel for people who want it, who are receptive and supportive and will benefit from it. Be selective. Do not feel that you must give a reading to anybody who asks. Your connection to your guide is a valuable gift. Offer it only to those who can truly appreciate you and your guide's energy and time. Channeling for those who are responsive and supportive will invigorate you. Channeling for those who seek it out of idle curiosity, or with a sense of irreverence may leave you feeling drained and increase your doubts as to the value of your work. You do not have to give readings to people who put you on trial to prove that you are really channeling. There is an abundance of people who can learn and benefit from your guide. We suggest you channel only for these people.*

You often teach best what you have just learned.

Let go of any preconceived ideas of how your guide will answer people's questions. His or her advice may be something you have not thought of before, or it could be advice that you had already arrived at yourself. The universe has funny ways of giving lessons. Sometimes right after you learn something, someone will come for a reading with your guide who is going through the same problem you have or have already solved. As you bring through the wise counsel of your guide for others, you may find yourself getting clear about things in your own life.

Truth will seem obvious when you are channeling.

Even if the advice seems obvious to you, say it, for the obvious is usually what people most need to hear. Sometimes what is meaningful to other people may not have any charge or meaning to you as you bring through the information. It isn't necessary for you to understand everything at the moment it is coming through. Your guide has the larger picture of people's lives and will only tell them the things that are appropriate. Do not worry or hold expectations about what the answers should be. If you cannot find a way to translate a message into words that are high or loving, use your common sense and don't speak the message. In these cases, you are most likely receiving a distortion of the transmission rather than the actual message.

Know that there is no right or wrong answer to any question. If you asked the same question of many guides, you might get many different answers. All of them could be valid. Each guide would give you a different perspective or way of understanding the problem. There are many ways to solve problems, many ways of looking at any situation.

You are not responsible for making peoples' lives work, or solving all their problems. When people come to you with their problems, remember that unless they are ready to grow, no matter what your guide tells them, they won't grow. Only they can change their own lives. Evaluate the quality of your readings by your inner sense and the process you see the other person involved in, not solely by the reported results. Some people may not use the advice of *your guide, and, as a result, not get the true value out of it. All of you have a desire to be of help to others. When people come to you with overwhelming problems you want to help them find ways to solve them. But some people are not ready for solutions, so your guide may simply lead them to the next step, rather than giving them full answers.*

Guides will not take away people's lessons, but help them understand them.

It is perfectly all right not to answer every question that people ask. If people ask you a question, and you find no answers coming when you connect with your guide, simply tell them that you get nothing on that issue. Even though your guide may have the answer, he or she may want your questioner to find out the answer for him or herself. Guides have the wisdom not to deprive people of the chance to learn by themselves.

Guides will not violate a person's privacy. They will reveal details about others that are beneficial for them to know, that will assist them in their growth, but they will not reveal anything that violates the inner privacy of another person. If people ask your guide to tell them what another person feels or is thinking about them, you may or may not receive answers from your guide. It may have nothing to do with your ability to receive information, but instead be inappropriate for your guide to reveal the information.

Some people are much easier to receive information for than others. If people come to you out of idle curiosity or without a serious intent to use your guide's information and grow, you may find your guide's reading turns out to be superficial. Guides give more profound information to people who are likely to honor and use it. You may also notice that your guide talks at whatever level people are at. If people are very new to their spiritual paths, your guide may use very simple terms and explain basic principles to them. If they are quite advanced, you may find your guide instructing them and giving them advice of a very complex nature.

Handling People's Questions

ORIN AND DABEN   *You will find that people's questions are often not as high as they could be. They may come to you thinking that your guide is going to solve all their problems, and they just want to be told what to do or find out whether or not something is going to happen. High-level guides encourage independence. They want people to use their advice to become even more self-sufficient rather than follow what they say without questioning. You may have trouble receiving answers to questions that demand yes or no answers. See if you can change or rephrase these questions. If someone asks your guide if he should sell his car now or wait a while for a better offer, you might change the question to "What will I gain by selling the car now, and what will I gain by waiting?" Slightly changing a question can bring about a much higher response from your guide. Help people ask good questions.*

SANAYA   One way to assist people in asking better questions is to prepare a list of the type of topics your guide is most interested in answering. Orin assisted me in putting together a sheet detailing what kinds of information people could obtain from readings with him. These included looking at hidden beliefs and childhood programming; what lessons and growth opportunities they were experiencing in their relationships; what inherent skills and talents they could develop; their ability to channel; past-lives that may be affecting their present lives; the purposes of this lifetime; the journey of their souls since their first earth incarnations; looking at growth areas; and looking at patterns, beliefs, and decisions around money and career. Often people who came for readings stated that they hadn't thought of asking some of these questions, but once they were aware they could ask, they did. People began asking Orin about profound and central issues in their lives. As a result, the readings created greater shifts and transformations for them.

Orin asks people to come with their questions prepared, and most find that just preparing them and thinking about them opens them up to their own wisdom. While he can help people with the practical and routine details of their lives, he would rather tell them about their life purpose, soul's journey, and how they may follow their spiritual path. Both Orin and DaBen prefer to give people information prior to their asking questions, and then dialogue with them during the latter half of the reading. Find your guide's preference. Some guides prefer to dialogue, others don't.

When people come to you for a reading, answer more profound questions in addition to the ones they have asked. Even if they haven't asked about them, have your guide speak of their life purpose and of their opportunities for growth in this lifetime. If they ask about a relationship, help them focus on its higher aspects. One woman asked Orin if her boyfriend was being faithful to her. Rather than speaking about that issue, Orin asked her why she was dating someone she didn't trust. He told her about her earlier childhood patterns, her relationship issues, the lessons she was learning from her situation. He showed her how she could change her patterns. He never did mention whether or not her boyfriend was faithful. With this information, she began to examine her past patterns of relating to men and decided to make some changes. A year later, she had let go of her former relationship and married a loving man whom she trusted completely.

ORIN AND DABEN *If people come and ask, "Should I do this or should I do that?" guides may take no position at all. One of the things they may do is lead people to examine the possible outcomes and thus assist them in making the choice for themselves. For example, if people ask whether they should go to the beach or the mountains, a guide might begin by telling them the conditions in both places. At the beach there is sun, the surf is high, and the road will be crowded. In the mountains the weather is warm, the trails are still wet, and the traffic will be light. A guide might then lead them to discover the essence of what they were seeking. They might discover they wanted quiet reflection and communing with nature, or that they wanted to be with people and enjoy the exhilaration of the surf. With this kind of perspec-*

tive and information, most people find certainty about what it is they want and which course to take. They also gain knowledge which will assist them in their future choices. Most guides will show people what they might expect, then leave it up to them to decide which path to take.

High-level guides help people discover more choices.

Some people ask whether they should leave their jobs and take new ones, or leave their jobs and become self-employed. Guides will probably help them see more clearly what each choice would involve in terms of lifestyle, skills, money, and so on, so they would have more data about their choices, rather than tell them which choices to make. Guides might tell them about other possibilities, to give them even more options. If people have too many choices and are unable to decide, guides will help them narrow their focus so that they can move out of indecision. If people ask, "What job should I be in?" guides may not tell them the specific form. They will rarely say, "You should be a manager at a computer development firm." Guides will help them explore what skills and talents they may want to use, what environment they would like, what hours, level of responsibility, and so forth. From this, people can draw to themselves a job that they love and that is nurturing and growth-oriented.

Guides may point people in the right direction, give many broad hints about what they could do that would bring them joy, but will almost never say, "Do this particular thing or that." We will often, however, give you steps to take to discover for yourself what you are here to do. We let you discover the form. We are here to lead you to a greater connection to your soul. We will help you shine more light on the situation and empower you, but with the concern that you discover for yourself your truth and path and the particular situation which suits you best.

Many people ask: "What am I here to do? What is my life pur-pose?" These are very important questions and issues. There are many reasons people are here. They may be here to learn to love more unconditionally, and thus put themselves in very unloving environments that challenge them to be loving. They may be learning about setting boundaries and limits for themselves and thus be constantly attracting relationships with powerful people who seem to walk all over them. There are hundreds of reasons why people come to this lifetime, and your guide will probably point out a few. Don't feel your guide must come up with THE reason for this lifetime. The fear that you can't channel the right reason or that you'll get the answer wrong can cut off your connection to your guide. Trust your guide to know what people are ready to hear about their life purposes.

Making Your Readings More Positive

ORIN AND DABEN   *Occasionally channels have felt people resisted their guides' information. If you encounter resistance, it may be that you didn't accurately translate your guide's message. From the higher levels, all things are said with such love and tact that resistance is almost nonexistent. This is how master teachers teach. Your challenge is to relay your guide's information with the same level of love, tact, and wisdom that your guide has. The clearer you become, the higher and more positive your own thoughts, the more your readings will increase in their love and ability to transform people.*

High-level guides
speak with love and compassion.

By letting go of your normal modes and habits of expression that contain hidden assumptions and implications, you can increase the accuracy of your translation and the positiveness of your readings. You may want to pay greater attention to how your guide phrases and explains things in a loving way. This will help you catch yourself if your normal mode of expression "gets in the way" of your guide's loving tact. You may normally tell someone "don't be so negative." Your guide may tell them instead to "be positive," focusing them on what to be rather than what not to be.

Use your skill in matching our transmission with positive words and thoughts. As you channel for other people, watch your words. If your guide sees a block, or something that appears negative to you, he will present it in a positive, loving way. In this way working through the block becomes a beneficial and growth-oriented experience for the person receiving the message. If a person is experiencing hard times, your guide may express compassion about what that person is going through, and then help the person see what good they are getting out of the situation and what growth they are achieving by being in it. They may point out what soul qualities are being developed such as trust, patience, or love.

If guides see a block or something that is holding you back, they point it out in a way that creates growth in a positive and supportive way. We rarely say, "This will be hard," or "You are not doing a good job," but, instead we point out all the good things you are doing and lead you to see how easily something can be done. Guides may be gentle, talking only of what you can learn and grow from. They can also be blunt if that is what it takes to get your attention.

We speak to people about issues they are ready to work on, and we tell them only as much as they are ready to hear. If people are not ready to deal with certain issues, we may not talk about those issues at all. We want to accelerate their arrival at the next step and to help them along their path. Although we can see many probable steps beyond that, it would only create confusion and resistance if we gave advice too far ahead of people's ability to comprehend or act upon it.

When you come back from trance, rather than going over and over what you said, worrying if it was right, simply review the information to see if you could have translated it in a more precise or loving way. Those who come to you come to learn and grow in whatever way is possible for them. People will gain from your guide's reading what is appropriate for them at this time in their *life. Remember that you will be opening and growing, and the people who are drawn to your channeling are perfect for your level of skill at the present time.*

As a channel you become a source of love and guidance for others.

If you feel judged by other people because of your guide's information, remember not to take it personally. It is a challenge and an opportunity for you to remain open even in the face of judgment or negativity. You are not on trial. If you find yourself channeling for negative people, offer them light and love. Keep your center and stay in your power. Their doubt or fear does not need to create fear or doubt for you. Realize that their reactions are ways of asking for more love. Often they want to believe and do so by challenging you to prove it to them. Their doubt is really their own voice of doubt speaking to them. Radiate love to them, and let them have their doubts without feeling you have to defend yourself.

SANAYA   When Orin comes in, my whole view of reality changes. I feel an incredible love and caring for others. When I see people through Orin's eyes, they are wonderful. To him people look like unique, beautiful, and perfect creations. He sees each person working as hard as he or she knows how and growing as fast as he or she can. Through Orin's eyes, everything becomes positive. One of the things that I find Orin doing is reframing. Whenever people have something difficult or painful happening to them, he will show them why it is happening for their good. Although he might express concern for the difficult or hard times they are having, he will invariably show them a larger picture of their lives. He will show them what they are learning and explain how they will be more powerful and evolved by going through those experiences. When he is finished, people feel much better about what they are going through. They have tools to move through their difficult experiences more rapidly. Orin provides me with continual assurance that the universe is safe, friendly, and forever concerned with our higher good.

Developing Your Reading Style

ORIN AND DABEN   *Each guide is different. Each guide has things they prefer to do and that they do well. If your guide doesn't want to do certain things, or doesn't seem able to do them, it may be that you are not ready to open to that level of skill or that your guide is leading you in a different direction. Don't invalidate your channeling because you can't do certain things. As most all channels have discovered, their skills continue to open and grow as their connection with their guide or guides grows stronger.*

As you channel for others
you will be able to influence
their life-force energy at basic levels.

ORIN   *Your guide may want to develop a framework for your readings. Both through the teachings of others and my instruction, Sanaya learned about the chakras. I used this framework for some time and then began with her to look at the entire cycle of people's earth incarnations, the overall patterns and interests of their souls, and why they chose these particular lifetimes. Her ability unfolded through several years of working with me. It required her to bring through stronger lines of electromagnetic force and hold more diverse ranges of vibrations in her body as I looked into these areas.*

Duane learned many of the standard bodywork techniques and frameworks of thought. He did his energy work using those frameworks until a new one began to emerge that went beyond them. As Duane began to see "density patterns" around the body, he realized that he was seeing the physical energy fields, the emotional body and the mental body. When all were harmonized, the spiritual shimmer became visible. He began to "see" into the muscles and physical structure, "knowing" where to touch and what to do to end certain kinds of pain, release past-life or current-life trauma, and repattern the energy bodies (the physical, emotional and mental) into their higher spiritual pattern. He began to see telepathic cords from others in people's body and energy fields, and found he could take them out, creating almost instantaneous changes in people's lives. By starting with a framework that he could learn and operate from, he eventually evolved through and beyond it into his and DaBen's own methods. Several bodywork students who were also channels have been able through their work with Duane and DaBen and their own guides, to see the same energy patterns and create many similar results. This new framework provides him and others with expanded ways of assisting people.

SANAYA AND DUANE These guidelines and suggestions for giving readings for others are based on our experience of how Orin and DaBen give readings. We are giving you ideas and structures to help you begin thinking like the guides do. You need not follow these guidelines and structures to give a good reading. These ideas about how guides approach questions are to help you as you start, but not intended to limit how your guide answers questions. Experiment, and above all else, trust your guide.

Process from Orin and DaBen
Tuning into Another Person

Goal: To channel for another person.

Preparation: Channel for others only after you have established verbal contact with your guide. Find supportive and open friends who would like to have a reading and want to meet your guide. Have your tape recorder with blank tape ready. If you wish, put on some special music. Find a comfortable position. In the beginning you might find it easier if you directly face the person you are reading for. Sit in a chair or on the floor, whichever feels best to you.

Steps:
1. Begin to breathe deeply, in a way that relaxes your body. You might want to imagine white light around yourself, ask that the highest possible healing take place, or ask that the most light possible be brought in between the two of you.
2. Close your eyes, go into trance, and call in your guide. Take all the time you need. Feel the compassion your guide has for the other person. When you are ready, your guide may want to greet the other person. Let your guide's personality, any voice changes, mannerisms, or gestures be expressed. Your guide might develop a standard greeting. Orin says "Greetings!" DaBen says "Welcome!" Most guides have ways of identifying that they are present.
3. Have your guide ask your friend for one of their questions. Particularly in the beginning stages of learning to channel, it is best to start with questions such as "What am I learning from this person or this situation?" or "How may I grow spiritually and bring more light into my life?" Guides feel free to ask people to elaborate on their questions or ask for more background information. If it feels comfortable to you, allow your guide to interact with people, for this also helps the questioner get clear on what it is they wish to know.

4. Let the answers flow from your guide. Don't expect all the information you receive to be astounding and unusual. While you are sitting in this higher light the most useful and often profound information seems obvious. Anyone who comes to hear your channeling has been drawn to you for what you have to say. Let the guide choose what to focus on and what to tell this person. The information may have no meaning to you. Trust that your guide will know the perfect thing to say, because he or she is aware of the larger picture of that person's life.

5. Proceed to the next question. Some channels find that their guides prefer the other person to ask all the questions at the beginning of the channeling. Some guides prefer to have dialogues. Pick whatever way is best for you and your guide. Trance states may vary depending on who you are tuning into and what information you are seeking. You may even find subtle changes in your trance every time you channel for the same person. You may discover that some people are much easier to channel for than others.

6. You may want to channel for just a short period of time at first and build up to longer periods. If you become tired, feel the connection growing weaker, or feel that you have answered as many questions as you want, finish the reading. Many guides have a standard closing line. You may want to develop one with your guide. Orin will say, "I bid you a fond good day." DaBen will say, "We will welcome you once again to these realms."

9 PREDICTIONS AND PROBABLE FUTURES

How Guides Handle Predictions

ORIN AND DABEN *You may believe that if you are really channeling, you will be able to predict the future. Many guides will not give predictions. The future is only probable, for what happens is tremendously influenced by your thoughts, beliefs, and unconscious programs. Any time you release a belief, change a goal, or develop different expectations, you will automatically change your future. We would rather assist you in setting up a better future than tell you what might happen.*

When people ask us for predictions, we view these as requests to help them create a better future. When people ask us to predict whether or not something will work, they usually have fears that it won't. When people ask, "Will I make money?" rather than telling them yes or no, many guides would rather lead them to understand what they could do to make money. By guiding people to hold higher visions of themselves and their potentials, we can assist them in creating even more than they thought they could have. We can help people become aware of their own truths, and release old patterns and beliefs so that they can create what they want.

You can create whatever you want.
The future is not preordained.

When people ask us "Will I get the job I am applying for?" the question implies that they are powerless, that they must sit and wait for something to happen. Often people's questions about the future indicate a lack of faith in their ability to affect their lives. As guides, we help people see what they can do to create what they want. In the case of getting a job, we might tell people to visualize having it. We might suggest that they link their heart with the people interviewing them for the job. Or, we might advise them to let go and trust that the best thing will happen, and point out that if they do not get a particular job it is because an even better job is awaiting them.

When a woman who has just begun dating a man comes to us and asks, "Will I marry this man?" or "Will this relationship last?" we may be able to see quite clearly that there is a strong probability one way or another. We may realize, however, that at this point in her relationship, it would be detrimental to reveal the probable future. This would deprive her of a learning experience. If we advised her that it would probably end, this knowledge might set up resistance and prolong the relationship beyond its natural conclusion. Or, it might end the relationship sooner than it would otherwise have ended. Once more she would be deprived of her lessons. We are very careful not to give advice that would interfere with people's growth. We want to help people move more easily and rapidly through their lessons. In this case, we might tell the woman about the lessons she is learning and the relationship patterns she is working through, then assist her in finding the higher purpose of the relationship. We would not tell the woman about the future of her relationship, particularly if her lesson was to learn to trust her judgment or to trust another's love for her. We might point out that she was developing soul qualities such as self-love and confidence.

If she were worried that she couldn't keep the relationship, we might help her understand how she could have it and point out *what she would have to do to make it possible. We may show her how to enrich her connection and get the most out of what she has. She would then need to decide if the price of holding on to the relationship was worth it. Sometimes holding on might mean compromising her ideals or living a less than joyful life. We will help her see her choices more clearly so she can decide for herself which path is right for her.*

High-level guides are very careful about telling people what is coming. If people want predictions, do not feel that you must give them. Things are not predestined to turn out one way over another.

SANAYA   When I started channeling Orin, he would not give any predictions. I was very disappointed, for I felt that all guides should give predictions. Orin kept telling me that he was a spiritual guide, not a fortune teller, and that there was a world of difference between the two. While he assured me that he could see what people were setting up, he did not want people coming for readings just to be told the future or what to do. Sometimes he would tell people of their future growth. He would tell them that they would be opening their heart or that their next lessons would center around communication or relationships, but only when this served them in the present.

After several years of channeling, Orin told me he wanted to teach me about the future and probable realities. For a period of several months, he gave me various predictions which came true. Several times he gave me exact newspaper headlines and dates, several months prior to their occurring. All the predictions centered around mass events. In all these events, he would point out that they were already being set up, envisioned, and planned by those in charge, and he was only projecting events by reading the mass mind and probable outcomes.

He told me that large scale events are easier to predict because they have energy lines from mass consciousness set up many months in advance. The psychic weight of these events, the mass agreement around them, the numbers of people involved make it much harder to stop or change such events. Whereas one person can change his mind and thus change his future easily, an event affecting many people is not usually altered by just one person changing his mind. This phenomenon facilitates prediction of major social events. Orin did add that people connect through their dreams and that mass events could be changed if there was enough consensus to do so. After he had made his point, he stopped giving me this kind of information. When it is appropriate, Orin will look into the probable future, but only if it assists my spiritual path or the spiritual path of the person he is talking to.

How Guides View the Future

ORIN AND DABEN   *The future is not a given. This is a world of free will. If you want to look at probable futures for people, ask your guide if it is permissible to speak of these probable futures. Before you do so, get an inner sense of rightness. It is important to check yourself out on this issue. If it does not feel right, if it feels like a struggle to get advice, or if you receive nothing, do not speak of a particular probable future. It is all right not to answer a question. Simply say, "I am not receiving any information from my guide about that question." If people's lessons were taken away by prediction, they might have to set up other similar situations just to learn the same things. Some people put themselves in the same situations over and over in order to teach themselves some major lesson. You have seen people who go from relationship to relationship, thinking that if the right person came along everything would be all right. Only after great effort do they finally discover that they need to make changes within instead of looking without.*

ORIN   *When I was first sending my guidance through Sanaya, she would often see that a relationship between two people would become richer and richer, or that it would not last. I was able to signal her with a feeling if it was all right to speak of these* things. If it wasn't all right and she didn't acknowledge the message, I would take the information away so she wouldn't see it and thus reveal the most probable future inappropriately. She would "forget" the insight and find herself channeling something else instead.

Change yourself and you change the future.

ORIN AND DABEN *In the reality system of guides, all time is simultaneous. We are outside of your linear time and space constructs. We see the entirety of the work we are doing together with you, while you only see it step by step. We are not saying that it is predetermined. Whenever you take a step or make a decision, we are able to project it into the future in all directions, and see it as a completed act, exploring all probabilities. Because of this overview, we are able to assist you in seeing the outcomes of your choices and help you find your appropriate paths.*

We look at the future you are setting up in two ways. One involves what you are intending to create, the other involves the steps you need to take to get there. It is very difficult to predict timing. It is much easier to predict whether something will or will not happen. If you have a very strong desire for something, if you are intent on having it, then it will come to you eventually unless you change your mind about wanting it. We can see the degree of your intent, the steps you are taking to get there, the clarity of your desire and many other factors, and thus we can be fairly accurate in projecting if you will get something. What you do or don't do could accelerate or retard your progress. To get something involves taking certain steps. If at any point you delay in taking one of the steps, it may take longer to get it. We can see that you might get something, but because your actions may vary, it is harder to be precise about when you will get your desire fulfilled.

The long-term future is much more variable and difficult to predict because the number of possibilities increases the further you get out into the future. The number of paths you can take between now and then increases. Each decision you make changes the ultimate outcome. Often we deal in probabilities, much like your weather predictor. We might see that there is an 80 percent chance that you will get the raise you are hoping for, based on your intent, desire and your relationship to your boss. We might also see a 10 percent chance that you will quit your job, noticing that you have had several thoughts in that direction, and possibly a 10 percent chance that you won't get the raise because of some other factor. At any time you can activate the 10 percent probability and quit your job, so predictions are made based on the probability of something happening. You act with free will to create what you want moment by moment. Sometimes a person's movement toward a particular future is so strong that it would take a great countermovement to change that path. It can still be done, however. You can change the future. Even the 1 percent possibility can always happen.

The further you go out into the future, the more you deal with essence rather than form. You may have the desire to have a fulfilling job. The thought of a fulfilling job is a thought of essence. The form the job will take, the job title and description are much harder to predict. We can more accurately predict what you will get in essence, such as the fulfilling job you want, rather than tell you what form it will come in.

The future is determined by what you intend to create.

If you were to ask us, "When will I meet my soul-mate, my future wife or husband?" many guides would be able to tell with a fair amount of precision if someone were coming your way in the near future. We can tell if that is your intent, and we can usually find the soul and energy of the man or woman who is coming. But you may suddenly go through a tremendous growth cycle. You may change your habits and tastes, and thus your vibration.

If you do any of these things, you will be capable of harmonizing with a different person. You may attract a different person or a very different experience of the original person who was coming.

Most people you are going to meet begin to connect with you at an energy level before you actually meet them, so that if that person has already entered into your energy field we can be fairly accurate in telling how soon you will meet this person, if it is appropriate to reveal this information to you. This meeting will happen usually within weeks after they have entered your energy field. People are often aware of this themselves. They may say, "I think I'm going to meet someone special very shortly. I can just feel it."

Sometimes it might be several years before you will meet a longer term relationship, and we can see a shorter term relationship coming. If we told you this shorter relationship was not your soul-mate it might take away your growth. It is more appropriate to help you see what you are learning and the ways you can be more loving than to tell you if the relationship is going to last forever or whether or not the person coming is your soul-mate.

Guides see your thoughts and emotions and can tell from those what events you are likely to set up. Sometimes you experience unwanted, unexpected events that you are certain you had no part in creating. But think again. Your universe is one of cause and effect. If you constantly think of yourself as powerless, as a victim, you will be victimized. If you often think how lucky you are, you will experience many "lucky" events. You attract events that confirm your beliefs. We can see the energy, thoughts, and emotions that make up who you are. We can tell from this the events that you are likely to attract. Again, there is no certainty here. You may change your view of yourself as a victim, deciding that you are going to take charge of your life or a certain situation. This would change the course of your future.

Any question someone asks about predictions can be answered in a spiritual way. If someone asks if they will be successful in their new venture, rather than predicting what will happen, your

guide can give them pointers on how to make their venture successful. When people ask, "Will I get married, will I stay married?" rather than telling them yes or no, your guide can help
them see what they can do to create the loving relationship they
want. Any question about the future can be turned into advice
on how to make that future happen. Once your guide turns their
questions into opportunities to help them create the futures they
want, they have served people in becoming more powerful.
Together you have elevated your ability to assist others in trans-
forming their lives.

Process from Orin and DaBen
Looking into Probable Futures for Yourself

Goal: To travel into the future and bring through guidance for the present.

Preparation: Do this process only after you have established a verbal connection to your guide. Have your tape recorder ready. Sit in a comfortable position and relax. Decide on how far in the future you would like to look; six months to a year is best.

Steps:
1. Go into trance, and connect with your guide. Imagine a symbol for the future you most desire. Let it represent your path of greatest light for the next year. "Throw" that symbol out into the future, and imagine it beginning to broadcast data back to you about how to arrive at that place. Turn your tape recorder on.
2. Imagine that it is now one week from today. Let your guide hold the light and amplify your ability to look into the future. In your mind, look at a calendar and mentally mark the date. Let all of your feelings and thoughts come through. What issues are on your mind? What new things are you planning or doing? Spend some time letting the images come to you, and record them on your tape recorder. Then dissolve these images.
3. Imagine it is one month from today. Again, look at a calendar in your mind and mark the date. Let the feelings, images, and thoughts that are associated with it come into your consciousness. What are you doing, thinking, planning? Notice the difference between yourself in the present and what you would be in your most desirable future. Perhaps you notice even more light around yourself as you bring the energy of your future self into your present self. Record your impressions. Now, dissolve these images.
4. Imagine it is three months from today. Look at the calendar and mark the date. Notice what you are thinking of doing and how you are feeling three months from today.

5. Follow the same steps, looking at six months from today. Then, as appropriate to the future time that you have chosen, go nine months, then one year, or more, from today. Imagine you are looking back at your present self and that your future self, aided by your guide's insight, is giving advice to your present self. Look at any issues in your life, and give yourself advice from this higher, wiser, and more all-knowing perspective.

6. In light of the feelings and images from these points in the future you may want to ask your guide some direct questions. Some suggestions:

    a. What choices and decisions can I make right now in my life to put me on the highest possible path?

    b. What actions, thoughts and behaviors would be appropriate in the next day, in the next week, and in the next month in following my path of light?

7. When you are finished, thank your guide and come out of trance.

Evaluation: People have found this process to be very powerful. You may want to do it periodically, and you will probably find your perspective on your life taking on a much longer view, more like the perspective of your guide. Look back at your notes or transcripts occasionally; you'll be pleased to see the accomplishments and the growth.

Channeling for Yourself

SANAYA AND DUANE   Some people find it easy to give themselves a reading, others find it hard. It is sometimes easier to start with questions that have little or no emotional charge for you, for your investment in the outcome might make it harder to trust the answers you receive. The questions in the Reading for Yourself Process that follows were developed by Orin and DaBen to assist you in learning to get guidance for yourself.

SANAYA   It took me several years of channeling before I did readings for myself. I found it took a very high level of personal detachment and calmness. If the answers activated a strong emotional response in me, it would break the connection. Getting specific details on my life also took several years of practice. It was much easier for Orin to transmit general guidance about my life to me at first. In the beginning as I channeled about details, I found myself getting so involved I would break the connection. It took several years before I could detach enough from the advice to hold a firm, clear connection.

Process from Orin and DaBen

Giving Yourself a Reading

Goal: To get answers on personal questions for yourself.

Preparation: Do this process only after you have established a verbal connection to your guide. Have tape recorder or other recording tools ready.

You may want to prepare your questions in advance for your guide. You might want to note what answers you have already come up with and compare them to what your guide has to say about the same issues. Some people jot down questions throughout the week so that when they sit down to channel they have good, well thought-out questions to ask.

Steps:

1. Go into trance, and connect with your guide. Turn your tape recorder on.

2. Ask your questions, and record the answers. Let the information flow, whether it seems obvious or unexpected.

Questions you might want to ask your guide:

a. What is the single most important thing for me to focus on in the next six months that represents my higher purpose? What is the second most important thing?

b. Consider a situation in your current life. Ask your guide, "What am I learning from this situation? How is it serving my spiritual evolution?"

c. How may I become a better channel? What things can I do physically, emotionally, mentally, and spiritually to connect more closely with you and with my own soul?

3. When you are ready, thank your guide and come fully out of trance.

Evaluation: If you have trouble receiving answers to questions of a personal nature, keep practicing. Your emotions or preconceived ideas about a situation may be very strong, and it may be difficult for your guide to come through your intense emotions.

Also, if you have already thought of the answers you receive from your guide, doubts may arise about whether it is you or your guide speaking. Many people find it harder to channel for themselves than for other people; some people find it very easy to do readings for themselves, and harder to read for other people. It is an individual experience; be patient and experiment.

SECTION III
STORIES OF
OPENING
TO CHANNEL

10 OUR CHANNELING EXPERIENCES

Orin's First Appearance

SANAYA People often ask me how I first met Orin, and if I knew beforehand that I could channel. I had not really thought of being a channel until I had a reading by a woman, Betty Bethards, who told me I would be a channel by the time I was in my mid-twenties and that channeling would be my life's work. At the time of the reading, I was 18, going to college, and it seemed like being a channel was a wonderful vision but a very distant possibility. I thought about it some, but filed it away with other dreams.

I finished college and got caught up in practical things, such as making a living. I worked in an office for several years, and later started a small marketing consulting business of my own. I loved the business world, but it seemed as if something were missing. About that time Jane Roberts channeled several books by her guide, Seth, which I read and loved. Several friends and I began to get together to discuss the books, and got a Ouija board to connect with our own guides. We got messages immediately, and asked for the highest guide we could get. We wanted a guide like Seth.

That was how I first met Orin in 1977. Orin came through the Ouija board, announcing that he was a master teacher and that we would be hearing more from him as I grew more able to receive him. It was clear that I was the one who was getting the messages, so one friend became my partner while the other took notes. We continued to get guidance from Orin once a week, and much information from another guide, Dan, who came through more often. Many friends came over for these sessions and we took over 200 pages of notes.

Later that year, I was in an automobile accident. A car pulled out in front of my VW Bug, causing me to slam on my brakes, which then locked. As my car was turning over on the freeway, time was greatly slowed and doorways seemed to open onto other dimensions. It was as if I could see into the future and know I would be all right. When I ended somewhat dazed and right side up, I knew a shift had taken place inside me. That night I put away the Ouija board and began channeling directly through my voice.

I remember my initial hesitancy about channeling verbally. I was afraid that nothing would happen or that the messages might trail off meaninglessly. Many friends were present and they sat expectantly waiting for me to start. I closed my eyes, and listened in the same way I had "listened" to the messages as they came through on the Ouija board. At first the messages I received sounded like a tape recorder going too fast. Ideas would zoom across my awareness before I could speak them. I asked for the words to come more slowly. Then they came so slowly that my mind would wander and I would lose the connection. But I did bring through coherent and meaningful messages and the evening was an exciting success.

This process continued for a few weeks, until the speed of the information and my ability to receive it came into alignment. The mental pictures were so vivid and rich that I felt the words were but a shadow of the essence I was experiencing. The ease of channeling the messages depended upon my energy and the amount of validation and belief I was willing to give to what I was bringing through. By focusing on receiving the first word or two and imagining that they were coming from the Ouija board, I was able to make the successful transition to channeling. Once I received the first words, the rest of the message would flow. I spoke with my own voice then for I was very shy about appearing strange to my friends. I would suppress the gestures and the voice that I knew were a part of Dan, who was speaking through me. Dan explained that he would step-down Orin's energy until I was able to receive Orin's higher vibration directly. Orin explained that my body was like an electrical wire that could only handle twenty volts, and Orin was more like fifty volts.

I learned that if I let my attention wander for even a moment, I lost the message and had to refocus my consciousness to find it again. Channeling required tremendous concentration. It was like finding a station on TV that I could bring in as long as I held the thought of it steady and unwavering in my mind. After a while, I was able to feel my own thoughts alongside Dan's. I would ask him questions mentally while he was explaining something to someone, and I could feel his reply to me even while I was channeling a message from him to someone else.

Still talking to me through the Ouija board, Orin suggested many things to help me increase my vibration and make it possible to receive him. The first time I tried to let Orin come through I almost passed out. I felt like I was expanding from top to bottom, becoming spongelike, larger than the room, but still encased in an energy field. I felt a crushing sensation in my chest, and a sense of power and love. My perception of light and color changed. I stopped trying to bring Orin through verbally, but followed his suggestions to get in shape, and started running in the wooded hills behind my house.

My breakthrough came when I bought a new tape recorder and sat down to make tapes. I went into a very deep trance and made a tape. When I played back what I had recorded, I realized I had channeled Orin verbally for the first time. The recording was a guided meditation for me to listen to on how to improve my connection to Orin and become a better channel. Orin taught me much about channeling. He counseled me to practice with a metronome set at the speed of a heartbeat, then to practice channeling at different speeds. He had me work with my breathing, practice focusing and concentration exercises, and many other things. It was at this time Dan left, saying that his purpose had been accomplished and that Orin would be taking over from then on.

The next three years were spent doing readings and talking with a variety of people. In retrospect, I realize it was a time of practice, practice, and more practice. My ability to channel clearly and reflect the messages accurately increased. The messages were instructive and accurate, and they helped people change their lives for the better. I was still working full time on other jobs, and yet every spare minute I could find was devoted to following my path with Orin. Being with Orin and channeling was so much fun that I preferred it over anything else. I experienced Orin as a very wise, loving being. He had a way of looking at the world that was definitely different from mine. What was becoming increasingly important to me was my spiritual growth and reaching Christ Consciousness. Orin became my teacher and guide into higher consciousness, helping me wake up to my own wisdom, and have more loving feelings and greater peace. He gave me many guided meditations to help me achieve my spiritual growth.

I met Duane in 1982, when he came to Orin and me for a reading. Duane had heard about Orin through a mutual friend and wanted to come for information about his life. His career for many years had been in geology/geophysics, in which he held a Ph.D. He was consulting and traveling around the world advising about the building of dams in earthquake regions and managing a large petroleum exploration company. In the evenings, he was also teaching and healing with bodywork techniques he had developed. He wasn't sure whether he wanted to continue his present career, start his own consulting business, devote full time to teaching and developing his bodywork, or to explore different parts of the earth, writing and looking for power spots (places that contain powerful energy).

Orin encouraged Duane to follow his inner messages and to try new things. The reading was about his life purpose and finding ways to pick what to do from the many opportunities he had in front of him. After the reading, I mentioned to Duane that I had trouble sitting because I had pulled some muscles in my back following a rigorous new exercise program. Duane proceeded to take away all the pain in a few minutes. I couldn't believe he had done it so quickly. In fact, I didn't believe it could be removed at all. I had thought that sore muscles and pain were a way of life when you exercised.

That was the beginning of an exciting journey learning about energy and the body, mind, and spirit with Duane as my teacher. Duane and I shared a common interest in many things and enjoyed pushing each other into new areas of growth. We worked together over the next several years, alternating roles as teacher and student. Working with Duane, I began to drop all my preconceived notions about what was possible in the realm of healing, particularly the idea that healing takes time. He showed me that it could take place with miraculous speed. Duane assisted me in aligning my body with the higher frequency I was bringing through when I channeled.

Orin and I were teaching the classes that were to become the book, *Living with Joy,* at the time he and DaBen suggested we teach channeling. By this time I had quit all my other work and was devoting all my time to my work with Orin. Orin encouraged Duane to develop his clairvoyant sight, and helped him understand the changes that were occurring in his bodywork.

DaBen's Entrance

DUANE My first experience with DaBen occurred during bodywork sessions. As I worked on people's energy, I found myself doing things that didn't seem to stem from any previous training or knowledge, and these movements and techniques produced amazing results. People found that injuries or pain they'd had for years sometimes went away in as little as an hour. I simply couldn't explain how I was producing these results. I seemed to "know" when I had truly finished a certain procedure, and I sensed an unseen presence that seemed to be assisting me. I wouldn't be able to go on to working on another part of someone's body until I had completed certain strokes and techniques.

This unseen presence was helping me know what to do, "giving me" methods of healing I had never been taught and had never used before.

I had been fascinated with the interaction of the mind and body, particularly after I became a devoted runner. The beginning of my running career had been punctuated by nearly two years of foot, ankle, and knee pain. Without too much hope, I tried to heal myself. I had been told that the cause was a bone or structural problem. As I tuned into my body more and more, it began to seem as if I could actually see inside it. I realized that almost everything that was going wrong was caused by muscles. Gradually I began to realize that I could fix my injuries by using my mind to change the way I thought about the injury, and then restructuring the muscles through physical manipulation. I realized that I could fix other people's injuries the same way. Athletes began coming to me. At first, I would recreate the injury in my own body. I would figure out how to heal it in myself, then I would correct it in the other person. After they left I would heal their injury that I had brought into my own body. I then began to explore ways to heal people without taking on their problems. One of the things I began doing was to help people discover how they could use their minds to heal themselves while I worked on them.

As I worked on people's injuries, I realized that I was sensing energy that was in and around the body, but not of the physical body itself. The sense of a presence nearby was growing stronger when I worked, but I rejected the ideas of guides and psychic healing because they didn't fit in with my scientific training. Being the scientist, I began methodically researching every bodywork technique I could find—from Eastern approaches such as acupressure and related disciplines to Western approaches such as deep tissue, kinesiology, sports performance, movement study, and a plethora of other bodywork styles and techniques.

A friend who was familiar with channeling and had had readings from many guides gave me the gift of a reading with Orin. I had selected Orin after listening to the taped readings she had from other channels, for Orin's information and delivery managed to get through my skepticism with regard to "psychic" abilities. That is how I met Sanaya and Orin. The reading really made me re-examine the way I thought about my life. I didn't believe Orin when he told me that I would probably quit my job, nor was I convinced that channeling itself was real. I deferred judgment, however, because I hadn't found any answers to my new experiences in bodywork through traditional approaches. As I continued working with Sanaya, I noticed a shift in her energy and aura when she channeled. I also realized that Orin's love and wise perspective exceeded that of any human being I was aware of. So I found myself faced with many contradictions between what I believed and what was occurring before my eyes.

A series of psychic experiences intensified the growing contradictions in my belief structure. One day as I was running in the hills, everything became moving patterns. The trees no longer looked like trees but like vibrational patterns, and I could see right through them. I was immediately concerned about my sanity. Not only did I not want to tell others about it; I didn't even want to admit to myself that these things were happening. A few days later, I pulled up alongside a car at a stop light. I glanced over at a woman driver, and, to my shock, instead of seeing a person I saw a cocoon of light and energy lines all around her body. I was so concerned that I asked for these experiences to stop, which they did. It was a while before I could bring them back when I later wanted to further develop this clairvoyant sight.

As I went on working with Sanaya, people who were channeling and sensitive to psychic energy started coming to me for healing. I began exploring the possibility of assisting people in their channeling through touch and energy work. I found that I could produce significant results by following my inner senses and the unseen presence that seemed to be around me. About that time I began once again seeing the energy in and around people's bodies vividly. I was able to distinguish three and then four qualities or layers of energy. Later, through close observation, I discovered these were closely linked with people's physical, mental, emotional, and spiritual auras. Some people had swirling vortexes of energy around them. When I was able to "calm" these down and put them into more organized patterns through touch, people experienced dramatic shifts in their ability to reach upward into spiritual realms.

I was beginning to feel a deep split. The scientific part of me went to work everyday to deal with management and the ordinary realities of science and the business world. After work, I came home and worked with people's energy, seeing things that science said didn't exist and producing seemingly impossible results. Although this "balance" had been ideal and comfortable for several years, the gap between the two realities was widening. I knew some sort of resolution had to be found if I were to continue functioning. My scientific self would tell me I was going off the deep end if I pursued energy and bodywork full time. My intuitive self was telling me that it could no longer stand going to work and denying what was becoming the most interesting part of my life, my experiences with superconscious reality. In April, 1984, I spent a whole day with Sanaya and Orin, hoping to resolve the conflict.

That day in April, I knew something would happen. Weeks earlier, the name "DaBen" had come to me while driving. I heard the name DaBen as if it had been whispered in my ear, and since then I had felt an urgent need to explore this phenomenon. I still wasn't sure I believed in channeling, although I could see the shift in people's auras as their guides came in. It was getting harder and harder to deny what I was seeing. I certainly didn't want to turn my life over to a guide, I wanted to handle it myself.

That day Orin had me say the name "DaBen" and invite the presence closer. I began to get hot and cold as I did. I started seeing Sanaya in colors and layers, and I could see right through her. The entity seemed to come closer and become more real. The physical sensations were very strong, my lower diaphragm was vibrating uncontrollably, and I was gasping for breath. It was very dramatic, and I realize in retrospect that if it hadn't been a startling experience I wouldn't have believed it was real. At that time, I believed things were real only if they had a degree of difficulty, and believed that if they were physically demanding they were probably worthwhile. I later realized that DaBen's entry didn't need to be startling, and I now connect with him easily.

My opening to channel created immediate changes in my life. From the higher perspective of DaBen, it became clear what I needed to do to make my life work. I had spent many months in indecision, being two people, wondering what to do. I knew now with a deep inner certainty that I needed to follow whatever my path would be in bodywork and empowering others and I wanted to learn more about channeling. The next day I outlined an exit plan and announced to the company that I was leaving.

It was a major decision, for I had to confront all the years of scientific training that had ignored or laughed at metaphysical phenomena. Channeling and guides were definitely not topics one discussed around fellow scientists! I knew that for my own sanity I needed to find some logical, scientific explanations for channeling, so I set about studying it as I had studied science and bodywork. Studying the body and energy systems from the perspective of opening to channel became my main focus. I also began to read everything I could find that would help me understand channeling from philosophical, religious, and scientific points of view.

From then on, Sanaya and I started channeling together. It seemed our guides knew each other. They often wanted to talk about the same topics, one taking up where the other left off. We received much guidance that helped us make some major changes in our lives between April and November, 1984.

It wasn't any one thing or event that convinced me of the reality of channeling, but a whole series of events. There was a consistency to what DaBen said. Even if he talked months later about a topic, he would take up exactly where he had left off before. He would tell me things were going to happen, and they did. Slowly, almost reluctantly at first, I began to be fascinated and hungry for the insights DaBen was showing me. I channeled frequently on bodywork and energy systems. Things have continued to work amazingly, and a trust and working relationship have now been firmly established between DaBen and myself.

11 GETTING READY TO TEACH CHANNELING

Preparing

SANAYA We want to share with you other people's experiences with their opening and how it changed their lives. While your experience will be uniquely yours, we hope from our and others' stories you will discover even more of the possibilities inherent in channeling for yourself. More than anything, channeling has been fun for us. In channeling, we have been following what we love to do. It has shown us that each of the moments of life can be rich and meaningful.

We were quite busy for the month after November when Orin and DaBen first suggested we teach channeling. We continued our once a month Monday night open houses and put together a schedule for the January through June period. The topics were about the Unseen Bodies: the chakras; astral, etheric, and causal bodies; and multidimensional selves. We didn't know that much about these topics, but Orin and DaBen told us that this was what they wanted to teach, so we were looking forward to these classes. In the midst of sending Christmas cards and putting together schedules, we were also planning for a trip to the Southern California desert to look for power spots and to continue our learning. We spent a beautiful few weeks in the desert, and while we were there Orin and DaBen gave us much information about guides and who they were, how they transmitted information, and how to know if guides were high or not.

Putting Up the Bubble of Light

SANAYA The date for the first channeling course was in late February. By January we already had more than the number of people we thought we could handle, so we set the date for a second course in March. Jean St. Martin, an excellent counselor and channel who I had stayed with earlier in the year, invited us to Dallas to teach two channeling courses. We were getting concerned about how fast things were going since we hadn't even put the course together yet. Orin and DaBen had given us the information, but they hadn't yet given us the processes. People were coming from everywhere indicating their interest in learning to channel. It felt as if we were swept up in a strong current; just keeping up with it was a challenge.

We compiled all the information about channeling we had received from Orin and DaBen, and bound it up into a book to give people at the course so they could use it to prepare for their opening. In between heavy rainstorms, we had some warm, sunny days which we spent channeling in the hills behind Duane's house, and Orin and DaBen gave us the processes they said would help people open.

A few days before the course, Orin and DaBen suggested we put up a bubble of light. They explained that the bubble was not to protect us from anything, but to transmute or change energy into a higher vibration. Anyone sitting "in" the bubble would be helped to go higher. They explained that we could create the bubble by getting centered and imagining ourselves surrounded by light. They had us play with the size and the density of the bubble, pulling it close, and then making it so large that it was bigger than the house, observing our inner feelings as we did this. They asked us to use the bubble during our Monday night classes to observe its affect on other people. The results were amazing.

The Monday night open house that month was on the topic of the multidimensional self, our larger self that exists in higher realms. Some call it the "source self." Orin and DaBen took people through exercises to help them go upward to visit the causal realm and even higher to discover their source selves. While they did so, Duane and I used the image of the bubble of light. When we felt the bubble was strong and our own energy centered, the energy in the whole room seemed to go up, people felt more loving and connected, and were able to experience much more. When someone was a strong doubter or resisted going higher, we would sometimes feel the bubble waver. Everyone in the room sensed and felt the affects. When the bubble wavered, they would have more trouble experiencing things or feel doubt themselves. When we were able to hold the bubble steady, people would find it easier to go upward.

We started "putting the bubble up" several days before the channeling course, energizing the room with images of light. We also began linking with people telepathically by sending them love and support, creating a "safe space," with the bubble of light around them. We have also found that having people put up their own bubble created the same effect.

We now had the processes as well as a book to give people, and Orin and DaBen said we were ready to teach people to channel. We were looking forward to the course, but the night before the first one Duane and I were nervous. What if our guides had been too optimistic about people's ability to channel? We waited with anticipation to see if people could truly learn to connect verbally with their guides.

People's Stories:
How I Discovered Channeling

SANAYA AND DUANE   The morning of the first day of each course we started by asking people how they had been attracted to channeling. For most people the idea of channeling a guide was very exciting and represented the next stage in their spiritual journeys.

It seemed to some like something they had been waiting for. Some hadn't heard of channeling or guides until a few months earlier, but the minute they learned about it, they knew it was something they had to do. This theme was repeated over and over by the many people who came to open to channel.

The people who came were self-motivated, self-reliant people from many different professions. They were scientists, doctors, lawyers, businessmen, professionals, as well as healers, artists, musicians, therapists, office workers, and housewives. Some people had encountered channeled information many years earlier and had put aside their desire to explore it more deeply until their children were grown, or until they had more time to commit to it. Some had been healers all their lives, working as doctors, bodyworkers, astrologists, or traditional psychotherapists. They had come into contact with the idea of channeling, and they had a strong urge to learn more. None of them had planned to become a channel; it just seemed like the next step. Many said they had felt they didn't "fit in." They hadn't been able to understand why some were here on earth. Yet, they all felt driven to do something. They knew they had a mission or something important to do, although some hadn't yet discovered what it was. They felt channeling would provide some of the answers they had been looking for.

They were all interested in growth and self-improvement. They had been drawn into the field by books, seminars, teachers, or classes. Some had illnesses such as allergies or recurring colds that conventional medicine couldn't help, and they had turned to alternative healing methods or nutrition for answers. This opened them up to a whole new belief system about what was possible. Many had found cures through changing their belief structures or healing themselves with positive emotions or a different diet, rather than with drugs. With this shift the floodgates had opened and many more new experiences and beliefs came flowing in.

Many said that they had first become aware of guides and channeling through Shirley MacLaine's book *Out on a Limb,* in which she talks about her experiences with channeling. As they read about it, it seemed as if channeling might be that something they had been looking for. Some had dreams which later came true or contained strong messages. Some had whispering inner voices that had become so strong they could no longer ignore them. Others in their quest for answers had explored Eastern religions, new age seminars and courses, and disciplines such as meditation and yoga. Some had read the Seth books by Jane Roberts and wanted to be able to connect with a higher wisdom and intelligence themselves, but had only recently considered that it might be possible for them. Some heard about channeling and guides from friends and found it struck an answering chord within them. Some had been studying with other people's guides and now wanted to channel themselves.

Many were in a period of personal transition, leaving long-term relationships or thinking about leaving them, or quitting jobs they'd had for years and moving on to new areas. Some were experiencing large internal shifts that they hadn't been able to explain. Many were questioning things that they had taken for granted. Over and over again, people spoke of being on a quest that they hadn't consciously chosen but that they felt compelled to continue, even though they didn't know where it would lead. There was a general feeling of excitement and adventure. Most people's resistance and doubts weren't as strong as their desire to move forward and to discover the possibilities that lay within.

Many were successful; they had achieved their goals and gotten what they thought they wanted, and still had the feeling that something was missing in their lives. Most of them had not been able to find the answers they sought within the traditional religious, scientific, or psychological systems they had explored. They did not necessarily want to leave these systems, but felt a need to enhance them in some way. Many were religious. Some were traditional psychotherapists who found they could heal people better when they worked with people's souls and spirits through meditation and other nontraditional forms than with the methods of traditional psychology alone.

One common theme emerged from all their stories. As soon as they decided to learn more about channeling, one coincidence after another began reinforcing their decision. Only days later a book on the subject would come their way, or a friend would give them additional information or the name of someone to talk with about channeling. Opportunities would arise to go places and experience things that would provide answers. It was as if some unseen force was directing them. Most found it intriguing and allowed themselves to be led on by their curiosity and sense of adventure. Most of all, they were drawn by the joy of growth and the possibility of reaching upward.

After hearing people's stories the morning of the course, we gave them additional information about channeling. We guided them through the processes that had been given us. Orin had them call in their guides and led them through the opening while Duane monitored them and worked on opening their energy through touch.

Later in the day we had them give readings for each other. People were able to do this with even greater ease than channeling on various topics of universal wisdom. They got immediate feedback from others about their readings, which seemed to greatly increase their confidence. They were able to give people information about issues they couldn't possibly have known about except through channeling. They found their accuracy tremendously validating. We finished the day with a group channeling in which all the guides talked about the purpose of many people learning to channel. This first day was followed a few days later with an evening during which people learned how to do readings for themselves and look into probable futures. Everyone had stories of their experiences and their changes, which we've shared with you in the next chapters.

We gave the channeling course four times in the next month and a half, and everyone was able to channel. Since then, we have given the course as often as we had people interested, which was about once a month or so. To our amazement, everyone we have worked with has been able to channel, and we have been elated at their success.

12 TEACHING CHANNELING

Stories of First Meetings with Guides

SANAYA AND DUANE   The following stories illustrate some of the typical responses people had when they first met their guides in our courses. A majority—over 80 percent—started channeling easily. Some had minor difficulties. We have followed the stories with suggestions of what to do if you encounter any of these problems yourself. The following account is presented as one course, even though the examples are drawn from several of the courses given over the last two years. Share with us the excitement of each person's opening to channel, for it is truly a special time, whether you are with a group of people, a friend, or by yourself.

The channeling course had been going on all morning, and the excitement in the room had been steadily growing. Both Orin and DaBen had been doing energy work to open and prepare people for the links with their guides. People had already learned trance states, posture, and position adjustments for better connections. They had tuned into the life-forces of flowers and crystals, and used sound, various chants, and other techniques to open their throats and connect them with their higher energy centers. Now people were connecting with their guides for the first time, and the excitement was intense.

One woman had tears streaming down her cheeks. All morning she had been clenching her hands and reporting trouble relaxing and going upwards. We had seen her relax more and more as her guide was called in. Finally, with her guide fully present, she was experiencing an enormous release. She said her boyfriend had just broken up with her and that all week she had been having strong feelings of being abandoned, rejected, and not being good enough. She had wondered whether she would find a guide because she didn't feel special or deserving. Her tears were tears of relief and joy; later she said she felt an overwhelming sense of love and protection from her guide. It was as if some deep part of her was finally relaxing and opening up.

Orin instructed her to tell her guide to help her release the emotional pain she had been carrying around. Her face slowly became more radiant. Soon she reported that she felt as if she were floating. She became very peaceful and her guide began to speak through her. He identified himself and proceeded to tell her many things about her relationship, its deeper purpose, what was going on with her boyfriend, and why he had to part from her. She reported afterwards that it was an enormous healing. She knew she had experienced a guide because all she had felt before was sadness, anger, and a lack of forgiveness. Now, she understood why her boyfriend had left her, and some of the sadness was gone.

Orin later told her that she had been preparing for this guide for a long time. One of the most important beliefs she had been working on before she learned to channel was her belief that she did not count and could not make a difference in the world. She had been working toward a resolution because a guide could not work effectively through her until she understood that she could make a difference in the world, for a high-level guide is effective and does make a difference in the world. Several months later she told us that she was feeling more confident than before, that she felt good about being out of the relationship, and was putting her life in order before she started dating again. A year later she reported that she had a new job, had moved to a new apartment, was dating a man who was a healer, and the two of them were exploring the possibility of teaching classes together.

If you find yourself feeling very emotional as you open, simply let your feelings flow. Open up to the tears or the joy you may be feeling. Breathe calmly and practice the relaxation techniques you learned earlier. After you feel calmer, you can establish a verbal connection. Ask your guide to give you more information on the issue you feel emotional about, or pick a topic of interest and ask your guide questions about it.

A large, tall man with a southern accent and a delightful sense of humor, who had had no previous experience in anything psychic or metaphysical, came to the course to learn this marvelous "new thing" he had heard about. He owned and operated several large real estate companies and mining operations around the world and was going to use channeling to help him with his businesses. He wanted to learn to channel because he was interested in growing and finding answers and was open to new things. He had gone through all the earlier processes with apparent ease, yet when it came to meeting his guide, he had trouble. He kept saying that reaching his guide was like trying to find a word that was on the tip of his tongue, something frustratingly close but unreachable.

As occasionally happens, his desire to connect with higher realms was strong but he had not yet found ways to reach upward. He had not meditated, read about metaphysics, or used his mind before to connect upward in this way. When Duane works with such people, he helps them direct their energy upward, sometimes harmonizing their mental and emotional energies through touch to increase their abilities to hold higher vibrations. Duane assisted him in lifting his energy until his guide could transmit and speak through him. For many people, we have found that all we need to do is tell their guides to adjust their breathing or boost their energy. The guides will do it or show people how to do it, and their channels will open easily.

As his guide began talking, the man began sweating and shaking; in time, when he found he could handle the higher vibration, these sensations subsided. His guide began telling him about how he could handle some practical details of his business, and he was very pleased. Although this man had trouble getting into trance during the earlier part of the day, by late afternoon he reported that the trance state was becoming a familiar sensation. His guide had a wonderful sense of humor and brought a feeling of playfulness to everyone in the course. He reported a year later that he had received endless assistance from his guide in all areas of his life and felt like he had found a true, caring friend. He said it was much easier to make business decisions and channeling had given him a much greater sense of compassion and understanding for others.

If you have trouble "reaching" your guide, keep imagining yourself going higher. Relax, open the back of your head and neck to a larger energy flow by imagining that you are doing so or asking your guide to help open this area. Practice concentrating on the thought of your guide, and ask your guide to give you an energy boost. Ask your guide to come closer and imagine opening up to this connection as you feel ready. Put on inspiring music and think beautiful, loving thoughts. Pretend you are channeling, and concentrate on questions you want answers to. All these things will help you expand your consciousness, raise your vibration, and come closer to the guide's realm.

Orin was working with a woman who was not yet able to bring through her guide. She had been meditating for years and was concerned that she would not be able to find the different space that was required for channeling. As it turned out, she was able to find the space easily. As she opened to meet her guide, she "saw" him far away sitting in a cloud and didn't know how to bring him closer. She was hesitant about speaking because she wasn't sure at first that she wanted to bring him closer. The cloud appeared to cover him. She wasn't sure her guide was friendly, or that this was really her guide. Orin told her to imagine sunlight dissolving the cloud, and suggested she talk to the guide for a while. Very tentatively, in her mind, she asked the guide to prove he was high and bearing good will. She kept an inner dialogue going for some time, until she was apparently convinced he was friendly. Then she let him come closer and closer until he was finally able to speak through her. She was obviously quite happy and excited about the connection. She had started a business as a clown, and she told us several months later that as a clown she connects with and channels her guide, bringing his love and energy to the children she works with.

If you see your guide off in the distance, as some have, get to know your guide mentally for awhile. Take your time; only ask your guide to come closer when you are ready.

A woman writer, who wanted to learn to channel to finish writing her book, was in a deep trance. She said that although she was still conscious of the sounds in the room, she was also quite aware of her guide and willing to bring through his guidance; however, she was having trouble speaking. Orin and Duane both worked with her. Duane began to stabilize her energy by working with various points on her body to help her steady the waves of energy she was receiving. She could have done the same thing herself by mentally relaxing her body, which Duane also instructed her to do. Tracking what was happening, Orin helped her realize that the energy of her guide was so powerful that, as she opened, she was feeling overwhelmed. So much information was coming through that she felt flooded and was only getting bits and pieces of various thoughts, which didn't appear to make sense.

The guide was transmitting to her in waves. When a wave would come in, it would contain so much information that she would feel inundated and not know where to start. Then the wave would recede, and she would feel she had lost the connection. Duane and DaBen opened some of her energy centers so she could handle the higher frequencies of her guide. Orin had her pick one train of thought and focus upon it. With that focus she was able to stabilize the transmission. We know that she did channel the ending to her book, and a year later she has three other books in process. Besides her writing, she is giving excellent readings to people and has established a counseling practice.

You will know the transmission is coming in waves if at one moment it feels as if you have the message, and the next moment it feels as if you've lost it. Ask your guide to steady the transmission, speeding it up or slowing it down as appropriate. Concentrate on the part of the message you have received, and begin to channel it, even if it is only a fragment. If after you channel the fragment you again receive nothing, simply wait for the next wave, and speak the "piece" of a message as it comes.

One man, a contractor, came to learn to channel because he wanted to change careers. He had wanted to be a counselor and was very interested in his own spiritual growth and in assisting others. He had not spent time meditating, but he had read everything he could find about guides and related topics. Upon connecting with his guide, he was unable to talk or move. Duane channeled DaBen to assist him, and DaBen found him lost in a world of colors, pictures, sounds, and lights. He kept floating, almost as if he were in a psychedelic light show. He had no sense of a guide, but a feeling of extreme well-being. DaBen began instructing his guide to adjust to the man's energy systems in a different way, and assisted the guide in doing so by touching various points. The man was using his inner eyes to see into the higher realms, but, being unaccustomed to seeing in these realms, was confused by what he saw.

Duane kept instructing him where to direct his attention, and his guide began to make the necessary shifts. He came to a place where he could see and sense his guide as a reality. Eventually the man made a direct connection. His channeling was excellent, and ever since, he has been getting good advice and guidance on his life. A year later, he was maintaining his contracting business as a part-time affair, while devoting much time to giving readings and putting together classes on self-improvement. With his guide's help he had uncovered beliefs and old programming about not deserving abundance that were still holding him back. His guide had given him processes to release these programs, which he used. Two years later, he has left his business altogether and is now supporting himself with a thriving, full-time teaching and counseling career.

If you feel caught up in colors, lights, and sensations, keep mentally asking for a verbal message. Use your will and your mind to keep yourself from getting sidetracked. While no harm will come to you if you get lost in the colors and feelings, doing so will delay your verbal channeling. Focus on a question you want your guide to answer, and keep your own thoughts on the question rather than the colors.

A sophisticated, well-educated woman came to learn to channel because she felt that she had been guided to do so by a whole series of events. She said that two years ago she was a firm disbeliever in phenomena like channeling, but now she was eager to make the connection. She was quite concerned, however, that she might be the only one who wouldn't connect with a guide. When her guide was instructed to come in, she reported that she didn't feel anything. Through DaBen, Duane could see that her guide was fully present in her aura. Sanaya channeled Orin, who talked to her, as it was apparent that she was intellectualizing about the process and blocking her ability to channel. Orin is able to track what people are experiencing and lead them out or through it. He gave her several questions to answer and told her to pretend she was channeling. With that suggestion, the beautiful, wise answers came in a much softer and more compassionate voice than she normally used. She kept reporting that after every sentence, a part of her would say, "That's not really a guide, it's just me," or "You're fooling yourself, you're not saying anything worthwhile." She had expected to feel an enormous change and be knocked off her feet. Instead she felt no physical sensations.

Orin had her answer in trance some personal questions about herself that she had been struggling with. Through her guide she gave very astute explanations that were, by her own admission, beyond anything she had conceived of before. Her partner asked her personal questions about people she didn't know, and her guide gave very accurate and insightful answers. Although at the time of channeling she felt that she might have a guide, when she came out of trance she again doubted that it was real. Her mind was standing in her way. Her guide was so strong that he was only transmitting a very small part of himself to allow a gentle adjustment to her energy systems. Her guide told Orin that she had much fear, and that if he came in too strongly to impress her, there was a good chance that she would not want the connection again. He wanted to err on the side of being too gentle, rather than too strong.

Orin told her to keep pretending that she was channeling and keep track of the information received. Throughout the day she continued to channel for other people, giving them information about things which she could not possibly have known. Although she kept reporting all day that she was just making it up, it was getting harder and harder for her intellect to rationalize all the accurate readings she was doing. She called several months later to report that she was feeling physical sensations while channeling and was finally admitting, even to herself, that she was really connecting with a guide. A year later, she still reports doubts, and says she has not channeled as frequently as she had hoped she would. She does report, however, that she has occasionally brought in her guide and done readings for other people that were astonishingly accurate. She says she is still working with her doubts, but she now recognizes that doubting is a major part of her process and that one of her major life issues is learning to trust rather than doubt herself in all areas. If you have doubts about whether or not you are really channeling, read the section entitled Turning Your Doubts into Friends in Chapter 14.

A woman artist who ran a successful fashion design company came to learn channeling to open her creativity. Her biggest fear was that she would lose control or be taken over by the guide. She was very independent and strong-willed, and she liked being in charge of everything in her life. She had been to Orin for a reading and Orin had told her she would be a good channel because of her high level of intelligence, her commitment to doing her best, and her ability to pay attention. Orin had pointed out to her that even being critical or judgmental could help, particularly if she used these qualities to develop a high level of mastery of channeling. He pointed out that her dedication, her desire to oversee and control things, her attention to details, and desire to succeed would help her succeed with her channeling.

She tried very hard to do everything the "right" way at the course, and yet a part of her was holding back, worried that her guide might take her over and control her. She was afraid of losing her identity and being "swallowed up" in the guide's identity. As a result, her guide was connecting with her very gently, not wanting to threaten or control her. Because he was gentle, she wasn't able to feel many sensations and thus wondered if he was really present. She was in a quandary; she was afraid of being controlled and having her guide come in too strongly, and yet when he didn't come in strongly she was afraid that she wasn't really channeling. Duane and DaBen assisted by helping her relax and adjusting her energy systems so that they were more open. DaBen also talked to her guide, and instructed her guide to assist her in opening her energy up, which helped greatly. Orin continued to talk to her mind, which was blocking the connection.

Orin told her: *"In many of those who become excellent channels, there is an initial fear of giving up control. Being in control can mean different things to different people. It can mean that there is an inner feeling that you are doing a good job and that things are progressing in a way that feels good to you. As a channel you will find it quite a challenge to match what you say with the messages your guide is sending you. You have said that you think your mind gets in the way of your channeling. Let us acknowledge that your mind is very active, very sharp and intelligent. You are skilled with words and your mind has the ability to see and hold inner pictures and symbols. Because of this we find it easy to transmit to you. We do not want to take you over, or to take away that part of you that wants to be in control. Instead it is important that this part have a different program so it can help rather than hinder you. We would like to have that part that wants to control everything watch very carefully to see if you are matching the transmission of your guide accurately with the words you are speaking. Furthermore, it takes a great deal more of our energy to control your vocal chords when you are unconscious, so we would prefer to have you conscious and participating as it requires far less of our energy."*

She began to relax into the feeling a bit more. Her guide continued to help her release places where she was blocking the flow of energy in her body. She had hoped for an enormous shift and strong physical sensations as proof that a guide was truly present, yet she was also quite cautious and would never have allowed a guide to enter if she felt controlled.

Looking back, she realized that she approached many new things in the same way, including setting up her fashion design company. She realized that her pattern was to worry and struggle with the process, even though the end results were powerful and successful. She kept working at letting go of the doubts all day, getting over her disappointment that the sensations weren't stronger, and letting go of the fear that they would get stronger. Her readings were consistently good and the information was of a high quality.

She reported several months later that she had some very successful channeling experiences and felt strong physical sensations and had more confidence in accepting that her guide was really present. Her business began to take off in the following months. Although she didn't find as much time to maintain the connection as she would have liked, things began to happen much more easily and magically in her life. She felt that guidance was transmitted directly into her mind whenever she asked for it, in many areas that used to require a trance. A year later, her business was so successful that she was frequently flying around the country. She had hired sales representatives and found success beyond anything she had even imagined. She reports that she uses her channeling for very practical things, such as helping her determine which lines will sell better, whether or not a particular trip will be profitable and worthwhile, and to help her discover new things to explore. She says that bit by bit, she is trusting her guide more, although she still wants to make certain that she is in control of her own life and not dependent on her guide. After she receives her guide's advice she checks it out very carefully with her own inner guidance, and only acts on it if it feels right at a deep level. She reports that after reflection it usually feels right and following the advice has brought the best of results.

A warm, loving woman who very much loved raising her two young teenage children to believe that they created their own realities, came to connect verbally with her guide. She was involved with museum and cultural activities, as well as many other projects. She had met her guide years before when taking a class in psychic development. At that time, she found herself writing information that seemed to come from a source beyond herself. She had been too busy raising a young family then to pursue this, but felt that it was now time. When her guide first came, she felt a strong physical sensation, warmth, and then dizziness. Duane went over and began steadying her. He had her breathe deeply and instructed her to keep opening up to let her guide come through. Within a few minutes she was able to channel verbally. Her information was quite good and she was pleased with the verbal connection.

In the next few months, she realized that she had an unexplored interest in doing bodywork. She enrolled in several classes and, while she was still involved in other projects, increased her activity in the healing arts. She feels that she is now in an intense spiritual growth phase, learning bodywork and taking classes in spiritual growth. She is learning all she can, wanting to get her work out to the world when she is ready. She feels the presence of her guide and the increased impulse to follow her higher path.

If you feel dizzy when your guide first comes in, change your breathing and relax to let more energy flow through your body. Some people hold their breaths or breathe with quick, shallow breaths without realizing it, both of which can cause dizziness. Channeling can often make you feel slightly warm and, if the room is too hot, this may contribute to dizziness. Breathing normally and ventilating or cooling down the room will help. In any event, the feeling rarely lasts for more than a few minutes.

Another woman, who was a weaver and designer of dresses of exceptional quality, upon meeting her guide for the first time reported seeing only pictures, images, and colors. She was concerned that her guide might not be real because the guide felt too gentle and soft, and didn't seem able to give verbal information. Orin told her: *"Your gentle, soft nature is reflected in the nature of your guide. It is the nature of higher guides to pick people to channel who match their own energies and who are on the same path of growth and light. Your guide reflects your gentleness, your softness, and your kindness to others. She reflects your ability and your desire to heal through color and form. She will be versatile. Besides helping you with your career, your guide will heal with a soft touch and a gentle word. Be yourself; you have your own unique path and your channeling will unfold naturally in its own time."*

It took her many months to find ways to work with her guide. She continued to see colors and images more than words. Because she was comparing herself to others who were getting verbal information, she felt that she was doing something wrong. She began to get very interested in color analysis and started studying how to work with colors, both in clothing and environments. She noticed that while she was in trance she could see colors around people, and eventually began to understand that various colors stood for various things. Her pictures, symbols, and images became clearer. Rather than trying to verbally channel, she began to describe to people the images she was receiving. To her amazement, the images made sense to others, and helped them see symbolically what they were going through. People were able to work with the images and create changes in the way they viewed situations.

She still continues to receive information in colors and symbols, which helps her in her work. She now advises people of what colors to wear to create certain mental and emotional states. She does color meditations to help people heal themselves, and is exploring ways to use color differently in her weaving. She says that her biggest difficulty was that she expected her channeling to take a certain form and come through in a particular way. It wasn't until she accepted the experience of her guide just as it was that it grew and unfolded for her.

If you receive images and pictures rather than words, start channeling by describing these symbols and images. Guides transmit pure energy, and symbols are often closer to their transmission than words. As you keep describing the pictures, you are establishing a stronger link with your guide. As time goes on, you will most probably receive the words directly, rather than pictures to decipher.

The day was closing and everyone had reached a guide and was quite elated, if not a little overwhelmed, at all they had learned and the new visions and potentials they were beginning to see. We were reminded once again that everyone is unique and that there is a variety of guides and ways to receive information. There are also many ways to open to channel.

By far, the most common initial block people have is the fear that it is not the guide who is speaking, but themselves. Because of this fear some people hold back from communicating what they are receiving. If this is your worry, your challenge is to let go and speak what is coming through you. Once you begin to speak and the words start to flow, the guides begin to take over and the messages feel less and less like products of your imagination. It is like pushing a car to get it started; once you get it moving and started, it is easy to keep it going. All you may need to open is simply the courage to begin, whether or not you feel that a guide is present. It has taken many people up to several months before they could *feel* their guides. People who have continued to practice channeling have eventually been able to feel the difference between themselves and the guide.

13 STORIES AFTER OPENING TO CHANNEL

People's Reactions After Opening

SANAYA AND DUANE We hadn't really expected that people's lives would begin changing immediately, so we were surprised at the many stories people had to share about how they felt and what happened to them right after opening to channel. We began seeing a pattern in people's reactions. Learning to channel required much concentration as well as the ability to hold a higher spiritual focus than most people had been used to. We are sharing their responses with you so you will know the common reactions.

One experience people have after opening to channel is an intensification of their dreams. One man, a lawyer, came to learn channeling because he knew there had to be something more to life than work. On a normal working day he mostly used his left-brain, logical mind. He wanted to use channeling to develop his creativity. He did well in connecting with his guide in the course, but that night he reported that he barely slept. His dreams were full of numerous ideas which revealed one thing after another that he could do with his life. Once the doorway was open, it was as if all the bottled-up dreams, buried talents, and resources began to surface. Channeling had created the intense connection with his right-brain, creative side that he wanted.

For some, another response to opening to channel is a feeling of let-down the next day, which continues only for a few hours or a day at most. This is similar to the letdown feeling people sometimes report immediately after they came out of trance. They don't want to come back! A woman who owned a travel agency returned the next day feeling depressed about her life. She said this was unusual as normally her days were highly focused on clients, sales, and other demands. She loved her channeling and was pleased at the level and accuracy of information she received. In fact, she hadn't wanted to stop, it felt so good. Now, nothing looked as good as it used to. We had her guide comment on her response. He replied that she had been setting aside many of her deeper desires, true needs, and spiritual growth by focusing on business matters that were not as joyful or important to her. When she made the link to her superconscious mind with her guide, she had felt as if she had "come home." Now, in comparison, other parts of her life seemed drab. It was like starting to wash a white rug. After you scrub one corner, the whole rug, which had looked clean before, appears to be dirty.

As time went on, she brought her outer world into balance with her inner life. She recognized that she had already experienced loud whispers that what she was doing was not satisfying and her deeper needs were not being met. She was always busy, and was not taking the time to listen to her deeper, core self. As she connected with her guide, she began to hear her deeper self as well. She restructured her business, passing some of the responsibilities on to a manager she had hired. She started taking time off and took up painting as a hobby. After awhile, she reported that many times the guidance seemed to come directly into her mind. She continues to channel and connect with her guide more formally to gain information in new areas, and goes into trance when she channels for others. She reports that she is less worried about the future and is simply allowing the things she needs to come to her.

Another kind of response, also emotional in nature, is the feeling of greater peace and contentment. One woman, who had been arguing with her husband because she felt unsupported, experienced a release the day after opening to channel from any need to defend herself or to prove things to him. She began to let go of her sense of neglect and forgave all the wrongs that she had imagined. Instead of holding it against her husband because he didn't talk to her or understand her, she felt compassion for his life and all that he was going through. She started acknowledging him and appreciating the small things he did for her that she had taken for granted. Within a few weeks, they were having their first honest and close communication in years. When we heard from her several months later, she was excited because her relationship had gotten so good she felt as if she was living with a new man.

Some people reported feeling tired or fatigued, and an inability to think clearly for the next day or so. It was as if they were runners who had run too far. Their mental and spiritual "muscles" were tired the next day and needed a rest. Channeling requires mental focus and awareness. Most people aren't accustomed to using their minds in this way for extended periods of time. The spacey feeling is usually alleviated by resting or relaxing, walking outdoors, drawing, listening to music, or soaking in a hot bath. Some find that being very physically active is helpful. This fatigue is a temporary reaction. As people continue to channel, they say they feel more clear-headed than before.

Other people felt tremendously energized after channeling. Some people said that the next day they wanted to clean out their houses and do things they had been putting off for months. It was as if life had suddenly taken on an added glow. Some people said they wanted to throw away clothes and other possessions that no longer seemed to fit in their lives. With the shift in your vibration when you begin to channel, things that represented the old you may begin to leave your life. Some people found that within days they bought outfits of different styles or colors than they had worn before. They wanted to wear things that made them feel more alive. Their old clothes did not seem to represent who they were anymore.

Another response is that things people had taken for granted suddenly seemed different, unusual, or strange. It was as if they were seeing the world for the first time, or waking up from a dream. One couple, who took the course together, said that when they went out to dinner afterwards the food tasted completely different. They walked around some of the shops in the area. The things they saw seemed unreal; the colors were exceptionally vivid; the people seemed odd. They felt as if they had just arrived on earth! Normal feelings returned several days later. They said they had had so much fun they would have enjoyed staying in that heightened state of awareness for a much longer time.

After channeling people began to really observe and pay attention to their surroundings, rather than walk around preoccupied most of the time. Others had gone to parties or social events during the next few days, and found themselves seeing people in entirely new ways. Meaningless conversation became even more meaningless and boring; whereas other people who they would not have noticed before became interesting. It was as if they were seeing people at a soul rather than a personality level.

Another common response people have after opening to channel is that they wonder whether or not they have really been channeling. (We have devoted part of Chapter 14 to this issue.) A graceful, athletic woman with three children who had channeled well and had a good connection with her guide, was overwhelmed the next day with doubts about the reality of her experience. She had kept asking her guide if he was real. As she was driving the car with one child asleep in the front and another quietly playing in the back, she felt a tingling all over. Then a voice began talking to her from inside her head, telling her about her future and things she could not have known about, which later came true. She came back to tell us that the experience was so startling that she no longer doubted that her guide was real. A whole new world was opening up for her.

Other effects may occur the next day, or surface after more time. Some people did not notice any changes the next day or even over the next several weeks; however, when they looked back, they were almost always able to recall events which were out of the ordinary. One woman told us that she had been planning a trip to the desert with a girlfriend, but decided to go to the

Rocky Mountains instead. She was planning to call her friend to ask if she would be willing to change plans, when her friend called to say that she wanted to go to the Rocky Mountains instead of the desert!

Many people began to hear from old friends and to resolve old disputes and arguments they'd had with them. Things that had been holding them back on an energy level began to come up to be cleared and released. One woman reported that when she returned home from learning to channel, a friend called whom she hadn't heard from in six years. The friend had abruptly severed their relationship after a disagreement, and resolutely refused any overtures of peace. The friend called the night of the course to apologize and explore the possibility of healing and forgiving the past hurts.

Sometimes there are physical changes, such as minor shoulder, neck, and upper back pain, that are responses to opening to channel. At the physical level, one of the reasons for such pain is that you are accustomed to holding your body in a certain way, and when you channel your guide, you often hold your body in a new way. The muscles aren't accustomed to this new pattern and will sometimes ache. Ask your guide to help you relax, and remember to adjust your posture so that you are comfortable. At the energy level, the reason for such pain is usually a restricted flow. Guides often enter through the neck and shoulder areas. As your guide brings a higher energy into your body, some areas may not be able to carry the larger flow. Imagine a hose designed to effectively carry a fixed number of gallons of water per minute. Suddenly you increase the volume of water flowing through it; the hose can no longer handle the water flow. It may swell up in some places and twist in others. If your guide is sending more energy through than you are accustomed to, it is easy to open to this additional flow. Imagine your energy opening and ask your guide to help you. Any discomfort will most probably disappear in a few minutes.

Some people have noted drops in energy, feelings of sadness, or feelings of emotional sensitivity as they come out of trance. Orin and DaBen explained that these are aftereffects of the heightened sense of well-being, openness of heart, and connection to the universe that is in such contrast to people's ordinary consciousness. Many people go around in a state of consciousness which they call "normal." They believe it is the highest they are capable of feeling. Then, when they experience the higher reality of their guide, they realize there is a whole new world of joy and expansion available to them. The contrast is striking.

We have observed that as people continue to channel, grow, and make changes in their lives and attitudes, the distance between the two states lessens and people begin to feel consistently happier and more fulfilled. Then there is no longer a drop in energy or any sadness after they return from trance.

Another reason for a drop in energy can be too much channeling. It takes time to build up to extended periods of channeling. A runner would not go out and run a marathon without building up endurance. Signs of too much channeling are tiredness after trance, feelings of restlessness, anxiousness, or feeling wired up, as if you had too much energy running through your body. Cut back the amount of time you spend in trance if this is the case. You can also exercise or do physical things that don't require intense concentration; these activities will help release your excess energy.

Over and over people would bring us stories of minor miracles, if any miracle is minor. A long overdue loan was being paid back. A house that had been on the market for a year was suddenly sold. A lost item of value was found. Some people wanted to explain these stories as only coincidences but, as these "coincidences" kept happening, they became convinced of the presence and protection of their guides.

SANAYA When I first started channeling Orin, I was only able to hold his energy for about twenty to thirty minutes at a time. A year later I was able to hold his energy for up to an hour. Gradually, I was able to channel for longer periods of time, and after much practice, up to hours at a time, with a few breaks. It may be easier and faster for you to build up to longer channeling sessions, so follow your own rhythm.

DUANE   I found at first with my bodywork that I could hold the trance space and concentrate from moment to moment for about an hour. As time went on, I found that three and four hour stretches of complete focus in trance working on someone's energy field and body were possible and even invigorating.

SANAYA AND DUANE   A majority of people start off verbally connecting with their guides and just keep improving and strengthening the connection each time they channel. If you stay alert, you will discover much richness to your process.

One woman, an accomplished medical doctor, had come to learn to channel to find even more ways to heal and help people. She had had many personal openings, wanted to expand in every way she could, and channeling seemed to be the next logical step for her. She believed that traditional medicine was treating symptoms and not causes. She was hoping that through her guide she would be able to see the causes of diseases—be they mental, emotional, spiritual, or physical. Although a recent arrival to these kinds of ideas, she learned rapidly and embraced anything she did with tremendous enthusiasm. From the moment she called in her guide, she was off and running. Her guide was eloquent and gave beautiful answers to the questions she and others asked.

She had come from another city, and when she returned home she felt somewhat lost. There was no one around her she knew who supported or even believed in channeling. She felt full of doubts and wondered if she was going to lose her initially strong connection. It was difficult for her to channel and she almost quit completely. However, she found herself reading everything she could find on metaphysical topics of interest. She wondered if she had let her guide down somehow, and called Orin to ask him if she should use her willpower to channel everyday. Orin told her that she needed to expand her concepts to be a better channel for her guide, and that what she was doing was exactly right for her to do to develop her channeling. He told her to continue reading as her guide wanted her to expand her own knowledge, and her desire to channel would return. A few months later she flew up for the advanced channeling workshop that Orin and DaBen encouraged us to give to enable people to expand and strengthen their initial connections to their guides. She was able to connect much more firmly with her guide and Orin advised her to channel for five minutes a day because at this point in her channeling development a regular connection would benefit her greatly.

She called a few months later to say that five minutes a day had become a strong, regular connection of a half hour. She was channeling much information on medicine and was beginning to understand the human body and its energy systems in new ways. She also said she was meeting people who were interested in channeling, and had given several successful group channelings.

She spent a year wondering how she could use this higher knowledge. Then she discovered homeopathy, and another shift in her thinking took place. She saw that treating people's physical symptoms was but a small part of the bigger picture. She realized that physical symptoms indicate that an energy disorder exists, and treating it at an energy level keeps it from becoming a sequence of physical problems. As she changed her practice to include these approaches, her whole life went through major adjustments. The last we heard she was firmly connected to her guide, and offering homeopathy to those who were open to alternative healing. She has been channeling remarkable information on healing and health, and we expect to hear much more from her as she follows this path.

Tecu—Sanaya's Guide from Another Dimension

SANAYA By the end of the first year, we had taught over a hundred people how to channel. During that year, Duane and I found that we needed to leave the city periodically for quiet outdoor places to work on our own energy and increase our connection to the higher realms. We took a trip to Maui that spring and spent most of our time there working with energy and channeling. Duane discovered a whole new underwater world through scuba diving. It altered his consciousness for hours and left him with a sense of wholeness. Having grown up in the Midwest, I hadn't had much experience with the ocean, so learning to get out through the surf and snorkel by myself was a major step. I loved snorkeling, and it was fun to watch Duane disappear into the depths of the ocean.

We usually channeled each morning for a bit, and we also spent several full days channeling. It seemed that the special energy of Maui, with Haleakala, a beautiful 10,000-foot volcanic mountain, boosted our energy higher than ever. Orin and DaBen told us it contained "power spots," doorways between our reality and other dimensions. We drove all over the island, sensing energy in different places and channeling to see if our connection to our guides changed with different places, weather conditions, altitudes, and environments.

I had quite an experience near the end of our stay, when another guide, Tecu (pronounced Tey-coo), made himself known. Tecu had come to me once before, when I was on a three-week trip to Kauai with a girlfriend. At that earlier time, he had come through every morning to dictate a book on how to heal yourself and others and discussed the universal laws of energy. Orin had encouraged the connection, telling me that Tecu was a very high being and that they were working together. I had had the book transcribed, and it contained very helpful information. Since that trip to Kauai, Tecu had not returned.

Tecu identified himself as a Lord of Time from the portals of the world of essence where all matter is created. He talked about other universes and about the worlds of form and matter. Duane and I found his information fascinating. Tecu was quite humorous. He said that he was from a different place than Orin, not higher or lower. He said that those parts of our world nearest volcanoes were the easiest for him to come through at this time. He spoke of his world, which phased in and out of synchronization with the earth plane. He told us that his connection was dependent on our being at certain places at certain times. He explained that it would be difficult to bring him in whenever I wanted because he existed in a universe with a much different frequency that only "phased in" with ours every now and then and only in certain places.

I found the experience fascinating. I learned that in Tecu's world, energy was symmetrical. He found the human body to be quite a humorous challenge for him and took delight in experiencing me walking. He wondered how I ever managed to balance the asymmetrical vehicle my body was. Whenever he tried to walk, I almost fell over until he got the hang of gravity and balance. The first time he came through me a year before, I'd had a sense of him taking inventory of my body, and sighing, "Well, it's not in great shape but it will do." Since the last time I had brought him through, I had changed my eating habits and gotten in better physical shape, and the connection seemed stronger.

When Tecu observed Duane and I eating, he was surprised at our system of nourishment. At first he seemed perplexed, and then full of amusement. "I understand now," he said. "Eating is at the root of your problems. First you have to have food. Then you need dishes. Then you have to build a house to contain the dishes. Then you have to go to work to pay for the house. All because you have to eat!" He added that in his system they just absorbed energy whenever they needed it and that it made life much easier. His sense of humor was so delightful that he would have both of us rolling on the floor laughing. His way of looking at our world made us re-examine some of our most basic premises and assumptions, all in a loving way. One day, he came through to give us additional information on the earth changes that he was observing and encouraged us to continue to teach people to channel, because it would help people adjust to the frequency and vibrational changes that were occurring on earth.

He has returned several times since we left Maui, each time unexpectedly, usually to tell us more about what is happening in the universe and give us practical advice on how to use the energies to grow and create our higher purpose.

Our Visit to Mount Shasta

SANAYA Duane and I took off part of August and went to a beautiful Northern California town, Mt. Shasta City, at the foot of Mt. Shasta, to work on this book, explore power spots, and connect with our guides more strongly. Mt. Shasta is the legendary home of the Lemurians and the Ascended Masters of the White Brotherhood, who supposedly live on the mountain. Many people have journeyed to the mountain in hopes of meeting the Great Masters, who are rumored to only appear to those who are spiritually ready. We stayed in a cozy home hidden in the trees, where we could write and enjoy the peace and quiet. We spent a few days camping outdoors, high up on the mountain, channeling, hiking, and running. Duane was getting in shape to climb the over-14,000-foot mountain, which required good mountain climbing skills. We never did meet these special beings, but we had a wonderful time with Orin and DaBen. The power of the mountain is such that we both felt a stronger connection to our guides and an increased ability to reach upward.

Duane was looking forward to his climb. The weather turned out to be beautiful. Starting from a 9,000-foot base camp, he made the six-hour climb to the top. From there he could see to the coast on one side, and to the Sierras on the other, each of them hundreds of miles away. He began channeling DaBen. Back at the house, I suddenly felt a tremendous surge of energy go through me. I stopped what I was doing and closed my eyes. I felt as if I, too, were sitting on top of the mountain and could see the view clearly. I had no previous knowledge of when Duane would reach the top, but later, when we compared the times, my surge of awareness and my feeling of being transported to the top of the mountain occurred at exactly the same time he channeled DaBen. The view I described and the place I saw was exactly what Duane was looking at from the top. We have found that through channeling we have a much closer telepathic bond. We have more and more frequent experiences where we are intuitively linked and aware of each other, even miles apart. Many other people who channel together have told us of similar experiences.

SECTION IV
DEVELOPING YOUR CHANNELING

14 CHANNELING— A GREAT AWAKENING

Channeling—An Accelerated Spiritual Growth Path

SANAYA AND DUANE People were having so many expanding experiences after meeting their guides that they wanted to get together regularly to share and explore their wonderful adventure. We began once-a-month meetings to provide them with opportunities to continue developing their channeling and for Orin and DaBen to answer their questions. From their experiences and the answers and information that Orin and DaBen gave in response to their questions, we learned much about the development of channeling and how it affected people's lives.

ORIN AND DABEN *Once you bring through a high-level guide, or connect with your soul self, you will be on an accelerated growth path. Opening to channel creates a greater link between the superconscious self and the ordinary self. This opening creates or accelerates a spiritual awakening. Your guides will be able to assist you with this awakening. They will help you experience more joy, more confidence, and more awareness of who you are. When you work with guides you will notice shifts and changes in your life. The changes may not be drastic, but over a period of months or years you will know yourself in entirely new ways.*

*Often after opening to channel
people feel excitement about
their lives and inner illumination.*

There is intense energy which is characteristic of any new beginning. It is a time of enthusiasm, insight, self-realization, and a
desire to change. People have reported that after the opening they
feel tremendous love for everyone around them. They feel a
wholeness and a oneness with the universe. They feel as if they
can do anything. Everything in their lives takes on a special aura.
It is much like the first blush of love. People feel as if they are
living in the clouds. They are caught up in a whole new way of
perceiving themselves and their worlds.

This period lasts for varying amounts of time. Like the tide, there
is an ebb and a flow after opening; it is time for normal reality
to be updated. You may need to change the job or relationships
you have. There may be personal issues that you need to act upon
and resolve. This updating process and day-to-day living may
seem like a drop in energy. Be aware that the process of creating
outer forms in your life to correspond to your new inner level
of light may not always be exciting. It may bring up some discomfort. But making the changes you need to make in the real world
will ultimately strengthen your channeling and connection. The
excitement will return enhanced.

There are cycles to a spiritual awakening like the waves of the
ocean that come and go. Some waves may be enormous and last
a long time. Some may be smaller and come often. After the first
stage of excitement, the next stage is usually one of integration
where the insights begin to go to deeper levels and merge with
the rest of your being. People who embraced channeling
energetically in the beginning may come to channel less. Now
that the connection has been made in certain areas, they may
need to integrate this new opening into all areas of their lives
before connecting again with their guides and going even higher.
They may put energy into bringing their daily activities in line

with their higher visions, focusing on making their lives work in better ways. Let it be all right if after awhile you are not channeling as often as in the beginning. This can be a time of deep inner change for you, and sometimes there will be outer changes as well. It is a time when things are happening from the inside out, rather than from the outside in. You are integrating a higher vibration with every level of your life. Sometimes when you work hard, attempting to find an answer to something, it is not until after you have walked away to something else that the answer suddenly appears. It is as though your mind has been working on the question internally while you did other things. It is the same with channeling; you may take a break from it and later come back to find the connection better than ever.

There is almost always a stage after the initial opening when the tide is out. You are re-examining and questioning your life, integrating your new wisdom; perhaps you are not even channeling. Be assured that this is only a temporary phase. When you are ready to open to channel even more, you will most probably find a deeper, clearer, and stronger connection to your guide.

Channeling gives you the tools to find your own answers.

Some people have expectations that channeling does not always meet. Initially some people think channeling will connect them with a wise being who will solve all their problems without any work on their part and without any attempt to change. Instead they find that they still need to learn their own lessons; they are still responsible for evolving and dealing with their own lives. Once people accept that their guides are not going to solve all their problems, but instead will give them the tools they need to solve their own problems, they adjust quite well. Channeling does not take away your lessons or opportunities to grow. It does allow you to see more clearly so that you can take more appropriate actions and accomplish things with joy and ease rather than struggle.

As the initial excitement ebbs, many of the issues in your life that you were ignoring, such as jobs you wanted to leave or relationships that didn't nurture you become intolerable; they may suddenly seem to demand action. Channeling points you in the directions of your aliveness and growth. Anything interfering with them will become painfully apparent. You will probably have a clearer picture of how you want things to be because you will have been seeing your life from a higher perspective and you will know what is possible. It becomes hard to deny your ability to create a better life, even though you may not understand immediately how to go about doing so. Difficulty is most likely to occur if you have been repressing your feelings and living a life unsuited to you. You may find your conflicts coming right up to the surface where you can see them. Remember that as they become visible you gain the means to solve them. Sometimes old issues resurface and, because of your new level of light, they can be more completely resolved and put to rest.

Initially when these problems surface, people may be tempted to deny the validity or reality of their channeling perspectives and experiences. We have seen the doubts, resistances, and criticisms become most intense at this stage. A part of you may want to go back into the old, comfortable, or at least familiar, reality. However, because you have been exposed to new visions of yourself, it is almost impossible to go back and accept the things that haven't been working in your life.

Sometimes people tend to be hard on themselves, even self-deprecating, for not having taken action and lived up to their new visions sooner. Be good to yourself. Everything comes at its own time. During this stage, people sometimes tell themselves they have no willpower. They feel they should be doing more with their lives. They may feel indecisive. Having experienced the higher realms, they may sometimes feel inadequate or hypersensitive to pain or negativity. Remember, this is an intense period of self-examination. Your personality may be comparing your new potential reality to the one you are living and find something lacking.

Some people feel that everything should be different after chan-neling. They feel they should be able to do anything without tak-ing into consideration their current situations, skills, strengths, and weaknesses. But, they discover that they still have their pre-sent realities to deal with. Some people are so energized that they bring too many things into their lives at once. They make many plans, take on new projects, get involved in lots of things. Later they discover that they only have so much time and energy, and that there is a need to focus rather than scatter their energy.

To varying degrees, we have seen these problems in almost everyone who is on a spiritual path. They are not unique to chan-neling. They occur in everyone who opens to superconscious reality and steps outside their personality to connect with the higher realms.

> Channeling will assist you
> in making the life changes
> you have been wanting to make.

After this stage there often comes a burst of creativity and in-spiration. It is a stage of doing, of completion, of finishing, and manifesting what you have wanted. It can often begin with the elimination of those things that have been keeping you from feel-ing joyful. You may have gone through a period of letting go. Even though at times you may still have mood swings and vacillate be-tween feeling high and confident and feeling unsure, you will generally feel very alive and in charge of your life. This is the stage where you begin to develop trust in your inner guidance and stop relying on the authority of others. It is not accomplished over-night, but as you pass through this stage you will find yourself strong in many new ways. It is like moving—the old furniture is being packed and boxed and the new furniture is still arriving. There can be confusion as the old leaves and the new comes in. But afterwards, when everything is in place, how good it feels!

Turning Your Doubts into Friends

ORIN AND DABEN *Doubts about the reality of channeling are common. Questions such as "Am I really doing it?" and "Is there a guide present or it is just my imagination?" occur as you first open. In general, doubts are protective devices, coming from the programs you've acquired from your parents and society to help you select what information you take in. You were often told to be careful, watch out, and be discriminating. Doubts can be your friends, keeping you from going off the deep end until you have explored something sufficiently to know whether or not it has value and is safe for you.*

When you reach the stage of your spiritual awakening where you encounter doubts, there are many ways you can handle them. It will help in dealing with your doubts if you understand why they come up after you open to channel. As the higher self becomes activated, the lower selves also become activated. We are using the term "lower" to speak of the parts of you that do not yet feel their connections to the higher creative intelligence of the universe, the parts of you that do not feel very nurtured or loved.

Imagine that your personality is composed of many parts—a wise part, a doubting part, a confident part, a loving part, a self that loves being the authority, a self that likes being told what to do. A delicate balance is maintained between all of your different parts. Every part has a counterbalancing part. The one that wants to let loose and play all the time is balanced by the self that wants to be conservative, to work hard, and so on.

There is a part of you that wants to grow rapidly and a part of you that loves stability and doesn't want anything to change. When you channel, the part of you that desires to grow rapidly is empowered. As a result, you upset the balance between this part and the security-loving self that has kept you grounded and stable. This security-self has looked after you, assuming that if the growth part got too much power it might let things get out of control and make too many changes too fast. This protective part may try to sabotage your efforts to go higher by creating resistance. It has many devices to slow you down, such as a sense of tiredness, doubt, or impatience.

Your doubts are trying to help you.

Sometimes your doubts operate to slow you down, keeping you from making the channeling connection as often as you might otherwise, giving your personality time to adjust, integrate, and catch up with all the changes you are making in your life. You grow at whatever rate is appropriate for you. Sometimes you want to grow faster than the pace that is good for you, bringing in too much light all at once. You have seen the physical effects of too much light when you have lain out in the sun for hours without adequate protection and gotten sunburned. It is best to get used to the light gradually, and give all the parts of you time to adjust. When you channel, you are bringing more light into your life. It can be a gentle, safe process. Sometimes your doubts may act like circuit-breakers keeping you from overwhelming your circuits. If you are channeling too much and are not listening to any other message to slow down, your doubts may come in to slow you down.

There are two other "personalities" within you that may find their balance upset by channeling. One personality believes in guides and has helped you to channel. This personality is willing to travel beyond reality as you know it. You have another personality which says, "I believe in what I can see, touch, feel, taste, and hear, and in nothing else." This show-me-it's-real personality gets activated in the process of channeling. It wants proof that the guides are real and can create conflict within you, causing you to doubt that channeling and guides are real. This conflict can occur if you are bringing through information that challenges what you believe in or stretches your imagination, or perhaps even if you are bringing through simple, practical guidance.

You ask your guides for astonishing information that will convince you that you have made contact with a higher realm. When we give it to you, you wonder if you made it up. When we give you ordinary, simple advice, you think, "I read that somewhere, I already knew that." It is difficult to convince you of our reality, for your rational mind can explain anything we tell you as something you might have already known. Be assured that we are aware of what you go through. We are not offended when you wonder if we are real. We simply send you love and compassion. If you could experience but a fraction of our love you would know that we are assisting you in every way possible, and we do not judge or find fault with you.

One of the reasons you doubt your channeling is that you may doubt yourself. If you are not accustomed to trusting your inner messages, then it may be difficult to trust your channeling, for both come from within. One of the best ways you can work with self-doubt is to look back at all those times you were able to believe in your inner messages and follow them, and things turned out well. If you are plagued by doubts, keep practicing. You will get small confirmations that you really are channeling as you continue. If you feel no energy around channeling and it just doesn't feel right to channel that day or week, then honor that deeper feeling, for it is probably trying to protect you from opening too rapidly.

To deal with these internal conflicts between your various "subpersonalities," you may seek out some of those things you did before, that you labeled as "not high" but seemed relaxing. During this period, people deal with their resistance in various ways. Some watch TV, space out, and don't get things done. They may rebel in various ways, such as stopping exercise programs, overeating or eating badly, or doing various other things to hold onto an old, familiar reality. They may feel as if they have gone backwards. There are many ways you can temporarily neutralize your expanding consciousness. Some of you may find that you need more sleep. Some of you may find that you want to do anything else but channel or work on your growth for a while. Do not worry if old patterns seem to reappear. Your security-loving, I-Don't-Want-to-Change personality is trying to reassert the old balance. Just observe the old patterns for awhile before taking any action to change them. Remember, these are frequent responses to opening up to greater levels of light through any process, not just channeling.

If you are doubting that you are really channeling, give your doubts a new role. Ask the doubting part of you to watch your channeling to see that you are transmitting the messages accurately and to make sure you are getting high guidance. Ask yourself whether or not you can use the information you are bringing through. The most important thing about handling doubts is not to let them detract from your joy.

You might give a name to the part of you that is resisting, doubting, or threatened by the changes you are making. Begin talking to it. Ask it what good things it is trying to do for you. You will find that often it is attempting to keep you in touch with your previous view of reality. It is concerned that you be effective in the "real" world. You certainly do not want to deactivate this subpersonality. Instead, you want to show it a new, higher vision of who you are becoming and enroll it in assisting you to get there. Tell it to help you use your channeling for accomplishing practical things in simpler ways.

Use your doubts as a positive force to motivate you to become a better channel.

To bring the voices of doubt, resistance and fear up to the light is not to give them undue attention. Don't make them wrong, be afraid of them, or give them so much power that they stop you. When you hear those doubts saying, "I am not really channeling, I'm not doing a very good job," you may want to stop and ask, "Who is that speaking, and what do you want?" Treat this voice like a small child who needs reassurance. It is all right to have doubts. Almost everyone goes through times of having doubts, even the finest, most experienced channels. You are not alone.

When you achieve a new level of channeling or another level of spiritual awakening, even after you have become experienced at channeling, you may find doubt coming up. The difference

*between those who become excellent channels and those who
don't, is that those who excel keep channeling, and don't let their
doubts stop them. Those who ask, "How can I be better?" use
their doubts as positive forces, bringing through better and
stronger connections to their guides. Your doubting side does
not want to sabotage you; it wants to find ways to integrate its
old views of the world with the new perspectives you are seeing
as you channel. Once you give your doubts a new role, they will
help you move forward rather than hinder you.*

SANAYA   A man who owned a chain of stores came to Orin for
a reading after he opened to channel. Even though he was channeling and bringing through good information, he was constantly
doubting its source, thinking he was making it up. He said his
channeling had given him a whole new perspective on his work
and his employees, and a new level of inner peace. He really
wanted to let go of his doubts, so Orin had him talk to his doubting part. He then realized that his strong, practical side was feeling threatened. It was the part of him that had been responsible
for all his business successes. It wasn't about to give up control
to this new, daring part of himself that seemed to be going off
the deep end!
    He asked the doubting part to carefully watch over his chan-
neling in order to make sure it helped him in practical ways and
to check his translation of his guide's information for accuracy.
The doubting part seemed happy with this new assignment and
the doubts actually began to leave. Orin had his guide talk to
him on this issue and his guide asked him: "Is it you or is it me
talking? This worry has gone on a long time now and it doesn't
really matter. Tell your mind to focus instead on the information
you are getting. Decide whether or not you can use the information. If you read something that is useful, you rarely question
its authorship. You accept it because it feels like truth within you.
Do the same with your channeling." This and the earlier work
with his doubting part created a shift that allowed him to continue with his channeling and to let go of some of the doubts
that had been nagging him.

Is Channeling Just Your Imagination?

ORIN AND DABEN *Channeling a guide quite often calls for the expansion of your imagination. How many of you have been taught to trust your imaginations? There is a widely held belief that the imagination is not to be trusted, and that only things scientifically real and provable can be relied on. Yet, many of your greatest scientific inventions come from the imagination.*

Learn to trust and honor your imagination.

Albert Einstein "made up" the theory of relativity. Then he proved that it was mathematically possible. Thomas Edison "made up" the electric light bulb and the phonograph, seeing them in his mind before he was able to create them in fact. He believed in the picture in his mind so much that he tried hundreds of times to create the light bulb and kept going even when everyone else told him it could not be done. Everything in your reality existed as a thought before it existed in reality.

Can you comprehend the richness of your imagination? Your imagination can link you with other universes. It can take you backward and forward in time. It can link you with higher minds, and create anything it focuses upon. The imagination can help you journey out of body. If you desire, you can project your consciousness and use your imagination to view places and people even while you are far away from them. As your imagination opens, you can travel into many realities. It is your imagination that transcends matter. It is one of the highest abilities you have. It gives you visions, dreams, and perceptions in consciousness that transcend your normal awareness.

Just because you feel you made something up doesn't mean it isn't real. Reality begins within you. When you first experience channeling, it may feel as if you are using your imagination. The imagination is at a higher vibration than the mind, and it is freer of the limits and constructs of physical reality. It is able to hold thoughts that may appear impossible or unusual to the mind.

Your imagination is the touchstone to the higher reality. Continue to channel, and use your imagination to express your guide's messages, and you will find yourself bringing through more and more profound and expansive information.

Your New Relationship to Your Body

ORIN AND DABEN *As you channel, opening up to a higher vibration, you begin to change the molecular and cellular structure of your body; you literally bring more light into your cells. You may crave certain foods or desire to eat differently. There is often a releasing and cleansing process that the body goes through over the months that follow your opening. You may discover a desire for bodywork or a change in your exercise or nutritional needs. You may desire to be outdoors more. You may notice that smells are stronger, or find that your sense of touch is enhanced. You may find a greater awareness of your body, and an increased ability to hear and understand its messages. The changes will be individual. Some people gain weight, others lose it. You will be redefining your relationship to many things in your life, including your body.*

*As you channel, you bring more light
into your body.*

It is important to bring your body along as you travel into these higher vibrations. You want your body state and your spiritual state to be harmonious and aligned. There is no set diet or exercise program for this. Instead, we recommend that you follow your inner urgings, and let your guide help you.

ORIN *When Sanaya first started channeling years ago, she decided to completely change her diet, going off sugar, alcohol, meat, and caffeine, eating only health foods. When she sat down and asked my advice, I told her with humor that I thought she was trying to accomplish overnight what would require about a five* year change in her vibration. With dramatic changes in diet or exercise, the physical vibration is changed and then there are no matching forms in the outer world to support that new vibration. Her activities, friends, and the way she spent her time all matched her physical vibration. As guides, we have seen that when there is too great a split between the inner and outer realities often the old ways will be stronger. Sanaya went ahead anyway with her health food diet, and within two weeks felt restless and uncomfortable. Nothing in her outer life felt "right" anymore.

She had two choices: to make dramatic changes in her outer life, uprooting everything, or to go back to her old habits. I lovingly told her not to feel like a failure when she went back to her old habits, but to change them one at a time and be loving and gentle with her body. Now, seven years later, most of those habits have been transformed into their higher expressions. (She still admits to a fondness for chocolate.) The change was accomplished easily and gently, one step at a time. You do not necessarily need to make the same changes she did. Each person's body is different.

DABEN   Duane has found that it is not diet that affects his ability to hold the higher vibration, but exercise and direct energy work on himself. He has discovered more and more ways to use our work together to gain control over physical energy and to harmonize the foods he eats and drinks with his body. Through this harmonizing he has been able to evolve his physical body without changing his diet. There is no one right way. Discover for yourself what your truth is and follow it.

ORIN AND DABEN   Remember also that you may not need to get rid of a habit. You may only need to transform its expression in your life. Your craving for sugar may be an expression of an unfulfilled need for affection. Go for affection instead of using willpower to stop eating sugar. Your need for a cigarette may reflect a desire to breathe more deeply. Smoking may be the best way you have found to do so. Don't simply stop smoking; pay attention to deeper breathing. You can elevate your habits into their higher expression. Habits are always trying to give you *something positive. Rather than make your habits wrong, ask for guidance on their higher expression. Once you find the elevated expression of a habit, the old form of it will drop away.*

One exercise we use is to have people imagine a clock. 12:00 noon is the starting position, 6:00 is midway, and 12:00 midnight is the highest, most evolved position. Close your eyes and imagine the clock in your mind. If you equate time with evolution, what time is it on your clock when you look at your physical body? What time is it when you look at your emotional development? What time best represents your mental development? What time is it as you consider your spiritual development? Notice where there is more than a 3- or 4-hour difference. Perhaps you feel your physical body is at 4:00 and your mental self is at 9:00. If you want to bring balance and harmony to your life, focus on evolving your physical body next.

One woman found her life changing rapidly after opening to channel. She was able to do something she had been wanting to do for years—lose 30 pounds! She lost it the first six months, without dieting. With the help of her guide she was able to run energy through her body which helped her lose her craving for sweets, and cut down her appetite. She said that for the first time in years she felt that food no longer dominated her life.

15 STRENGTHENING YOUR CHANNELING

How Often Do You Channel?

ORIN AND DABEN *Many of you ask how regularly you should channel to develop a strong and clear connection to your guide. "Regularly" can be defined as a session once a week or a few minutes every day. It can also be working on a project for many hours at a time during scheduled periods. Do not make it a "should" or "have to." Channel as often and as long as it feels good. Above all, follow your inner joy. As you open up to the higher realms, you will probably feel a desire to channel deep within you. If you find you aren't channeling as often as you'd like, it is possible to use your will and make yourself practice all the time, but we find that the most lasting results come from channeling when it feels joyful and useful to you. Some people have found that as little as five minutes three or four times a week keeps the connection strong and provides them with ongoing, practical guidance.*

There will be days when the connection is strong and you are open and receptive. The messages will seem to flow freely and inspire you. At other times you may find it harder to make the connection; the reception may feel hazy, unclear, or the ideas just won't come. There are many factors at work here, so don't blame yourself, even if days go by and the connection is hard

to establish. Transmission can vary. When the connection is difficult to establish, turn your attention to something else for
awhile. You may need a change of scenery, more exercise, more
sleep. You may simply need to take a break for awhile. Sometimes
there are "magnetic storms" or interferences in our realms that
make the connection weak. If you find it difficult to channel, do
it again at other times.

> ## People experience channeling as
> ## a sudden inflow of ideas, insights,
> ## creativity, and clear guidance.

You may find yourself easily going into a channeling space while
you are doing things that bring relaxation or heightened
awareness. It is always under your control. This could happen
when you are exercising, running, taking a shower, listening to
music, cooking dinner, watching TV, praying, or meditating. Some
of the easiest times for you to connect with either your guide
or your own inner knowingness are when you feel relaxed and
at peace.

DUANE   In the beginning I found it was best to connect with
DaBen for only a little bit at a time. This allowed me to adjust
to the physical and personality changes channeling brought about
in regular, small increments without overloading. I carried a tape
recorder, and if I had to wait before a meeting, I would spend
five minutes channeling. DaBen would continue to channel on
whatever topic he had been channeling on the time before. I
found that using channeling on everyday things was one way to
increase my connection. I also channeled in sessions of about
a half-hour several times a week to bring through information
of a scientific nature. Sometimes I would pick a topic that I knew
a lot about, think about it myself, then ask DaBen questions about
the same topic. As I channeled, DaBen would give me a new
perspective; I would learn something that I had not thought about

before. This helped strengthen the connection and helped me believe that my channeling had real value.

Strengthening the Connection

ORIN AND DABEN   *To increase your connection to your guide, you can consciously think of your guide or your guide's name. You need not do more that this to bring your guide's light and love to you. You can also learn to call in your guide for brief moments by closing your eyes and asking for guidance and getting simple yes or no impressions instantly. You can do this whether you are standing in the grocery store line, driving your car or walking down the street. You can bring the essence of your connection with your guide through at any given time for however long you want—be it thirty seconds or three minutes. This type of connection does not need to be a lengthy process. One of the benefits of learning how to channel by making this type of connection without going into a formal trance state is that you can use it in your office, for meetings, in public, in fact, almost anywhere and anytime you need an additional source of inspiration or guidance.*

As you continue to channel, you will find your ability to connect with and bring through new levels of wisdom increasing. You will experience a continual series of shifts throughout your channeling development. As you become more and more accustomed to the higher realms, learning to travel into them and expanding your vibration to connect with them, and as your channel becomes more open, you can bring through more power at a pure energy level.

When people have gone to a new level in their channeling, they sometimes experience nervousness afterwards. This can happen even to experienced channels. When the transition is made to an even higher vibration, it triggers a process of growth that is sometimes like the first opening. The nervousness is usually due to more energy coming in through your body than you are used to.

> *You don't have to be in a good mood*
> *to channel, just willing to be.*

It is possible to reach your guide even in the middle of an emotional crisis or upset. You do have to be willing to be in a good mood, however, for once you channel you will have trouble hanging on to your upset. From your guide's perspective you will most likely see both people's point of view, or understand what you are learning from a situation and your part in creating it. From this higher, more loving view, it is hard to stay angry and closed.

Receiving More Specific Information

ORIN AND DABEN   *You can get more specific answers by having people ask more specific questions, or clarifying what it is they want to know. When people have general requests, such as "Tell me about John," many guides would ask what relationship John is to them, and what specifically they want to know about him. If someone says, "Tell me about my job," a guide might ask, "What do you specifically want to know about your job?" Getting specific information also often depends upon your ability to relax and trust the messages you are receiving.*

> *Guides practice economy of energy.*

Guides practice economy of energy. We do things simply, with the least expenditure of energy. We might be able to see everything about a person or their job, but it would take hours to talk about it. It is much faster and saves much of our energy to get the questioner to be specific about what he or she wants to know, and ask just that question. This also serves people by helping them see clearly what the issues really are. A good way to get more detailed, specific answers is to have people tell your guide exactly what they want to know about.

Another challenge is your trust in relaying detailed information. Your mind often gets in the way. You may get very concrete *advice from your guide, and still have trouble relaying it because of your fear that it might be wrong. This is one of the blocks to being specific. Remember that you usually receive channeling in your right-brain, and relay information from your left-brain, so your skill as a translator is important in accurately passing on detailed information. General, non-specific information is much easier to receive at first, and it is through practice and trust that you will become more skilled at details.*

SANAYA When I first began channeling Orin, I was concerned that his information be useful and valuable to people. The many positive reports from people who came for readings gave me confidence in the accuracy and value of Orin's specific advice about life purpose and direction. However, Orin sometimes gave a person very detailed information—about their relationships, a new home, an upcoming vacation, and other things I couldn't have known anything about. I worried about the accuracy of the details that Orin was giving others, and sometimes I would stop speaking. Like the wisdom people reported in the general advice about life purpose, I learned that Orin's details were also accurate, and I slowly began to trust them. In retrospect, I don't know why I worried so much. From my own perspective at the time, I didn't know if the details were right or wrong so it took a lot of trust to relay whatever I was receiving.

Now I easily relay what I receive from Orin. The information comes so rapidly I rarely know what he is going to say before it is spoken. His messages are transmitted to me and said through my voice a split second before I can think about them. Orin didn't transmit this way until I had built up a lot of trust in the accuracy of the messages and was willing to let them be spoken without first checking out each sentence. I couldn't add to or change his messages, but I could stop speaking and cut off the information. Remember conscious, as opposed to unconscious, channeling provides you the opportunity to learn as you channel. Conscious channeling also gives you both the challenge of letting the messages flow and the responsibility for accurately relaying your guide's messages.

DUANE When DaBen first came, I told him "I'll handle the details of my life; I don't want any interference from you." DaBen was wonderful at giving me scientific information, explaining earth changes, and talking about general theories. After a few months, I wanted DaBen to give me detailed advice about a business decision, but he wouldn't do it. I began to think that I didn't have a clear connection, and worried about my inability to get details about my life. After six months of trying to get specific, personal information, I asked DaBen what the problem was. He told me that I had requested that he *not* give me details and specifics, and he was following my directive. I told him that I had changed my mind, that I now wanted personal guidance and specific information. After that he was wonderful at offering advice and suggestions on very specific things. In my experience, guides honor your personal boundaries and requests. They go to great lengths to respect you and your life.

Other Ways Your Guide Reaches You

ORIN AND DABEN *We have other ways of getting more specific information to you besides having you channel it. We do not waste valuable energy. Everything we do is accomplished in the easiest possible way, so that all of our available energy may be used to the highest good.*

Guides have many ways to reach you.

You may find that after you channel information, a related book comes your way or people come to you and begin to talk about what you have just been receiving. When Duane and Sanaya were channeling information about earth changes, every time they reached a part that required extensive explanations, a book would be given to them within a few days which would elaborate on the theme, clarifying and validating the information they had channeled. The book provided the data they needed, saving them hours of channeling.

We may send you a greeting in the way of a rainbow or a special crystal. The lyrics of a song you just heard on the radio may seem to speak directly to your heart. You may have a dream with an answer in it. A class or teacher may help you find the answer. Guides have many ways to reach you.

Will Channeling Help You Win the Lottery?

ORIN AND DABEN *Psychic and extrasensory abilities used in predicting numbers and events are different from channeling. There are seven centers of energy, called "chakras." They are focused partly within the physical body. The first chakra is at the base of the spine and the seventh chakra is at the top of your head, with the others in between. The psychic center, the sixth chakra, has been called the "third eye," and is located between your eyebrows. Psychic abilities come from using this sixth chakra, or third eye. In channeling you are receiving guidance from the seventh chakra, called the "Crown Center." As you open your seventh chakra, you build the bridge to the higher realms, for this center is associated with spiritual awakening. This center also deals with imagination, fantasy, and visions. This is why you may feel that you are "making things up" when you are in a channeling space. You open this center by asking for guidance on your higher purpose and by using your channeling to enrich and empower your life. Live the higher ideals, and be responsible, honest, and come from your integrity in all that you do.*

You do not need to develop your psychic abilities to become a good channel.

Your sixth chakra, the psychic center, deals with clairvoyance, precognition, telepathy, remote viewing (the ability to see things happening far away when you are not physically present), and similar skills. As you channel, you may experience the awaken-

ing of your psychic abilities, but we encourage you to open your crown center, which is your spiritual center, as your main focus. Telepathy, clairvoyance, and intuition are skills that may develop as you channel, but can also be developed without learning to channel.

SANAYA AND DUANE   One thing we have observed over and over is that using the guides for predicting winners at the horse races or numbers on the roulette wheel rarely works. Our guides have told us that high guides are here for our spiritual enrichment, and that obtaining money by gambling is simply not of interest to them. Even people who wish to use the money they gain for good works find that money usually comes to them through their spiritual endeavors that directly help others, rather than through a lucky roll of the dice or turn of the wheel.

Channeling is a connection to the higher realms, and it is best to focus on connecting with a high-level guide rather than developing your psychic abilities. These abilities will unfold in their time, if they are of spiritual value to you. High level guides work only with those who use their channeling for spiritual growth. However, it is likely that in following your spiritual path you will be financially prosperous as well.

Can You Change Guides?

SANAYA AND DUANE   It is not uncommon for one guide to work with you initially and for another to come in later. You may connect with a higher guide, or with a higher part of your original guide, or it may be that your direction has changed, and it is time to work with another kind of guide. This is not to say that the guide you have been channeling is inadequate, but he or she may be stepping down the vibration of an even higher guide until you are physically, mentally, and emotionally able to handle an even finer frequency. Some of you may also work with several guides at one time, each one having a different area of expertise.

There are many ways to first become aware of a new guide. Your trance state may feel different, lighter or deeper. Your voice may begin to change, becoming lower, deeper, or taking on an accent. The communications of your guide may be of a different nature than in the past. Your guide may feel wiser or be able to give you an even larger perspective.

One night a woman who had been channeling a guide for years found herself bringing through what seemed to be a new guide. The vibration of this new guide was so high that everyone around had many deep insights and felt many shifts within. She asked her familiar guide afterwards if she had channeled a new guide, and he told her, no, that she had connected with a much greater part of his energy than before. He hadn't been able to bring through this part of himself in the past because of her earlier resistance to all the power that came with this expansion.

About 10 percent of the people who have learned to channel a guide through our courses have changed guides within the first year. Many of them had a feeling in the beginning that their first guide would not be their permanent guide. Some began to notice a shift after months of regular practice. It often started with a feeling of restlessness or frustration with their channeling. New levels of information seemed just out of their reach. Almost all felt a change of some sort or a premonition that something was different before the new guide came through. If you wonder whether a new guide is present, ask. Guides will tell you who they are and what is happening.

One woman called excitedly to tell us of her new guide. She had enjoyed her first guide, but felt the connection was weak and still had many doubts about the realness of this guide. She met regularly with a group of people who had also taken the course. Suddenly one night as she went into trance, a booming, strong male voice came out. He announced that he was her new guide, and it was time for their work together to begin. He gave her clear instructions about her next steps. He was very concise, amusing, and firm in his advice. Everyone loved him, and he has been with her ever since. She is thrilled with the quality of her readings. Her old guide is gone, having served to open the doorway for her new guide.

DaBen often has other guides assist him. DaBen assists Duane with his energy and bodywork, and likes to speak of scientific matters. He is able with his voice and energy to take people "traveling" mentally into other dimensions to explore new experiences of themselves. However, when certain specific information is requested, DaBen calls on what he refers to as his "filters." DaBen will still be present, managing the energy, but a "filter" will relay the information to Duane.

Channeling the Same Guide as Others

ORIN   *People often ask if more than one person can channel the same guide. Some guides do come through several people, although they will have slightly different tones and messages as they do. Channels in the Michael group, for instance, say they are all channeling "Michael," a collective higher consciousness of a thousand entities.*

Many people feel that they are channeling Orin. I will say that I do come through other people, but I would not identify myself as Orin, for Orin is the "identity band" I use to signify my energy as it comes through Sanaya. My energy will come through each channel in a slightly different way, and I will use a different name to create a different "identity band" signification. Of course, it is possible for another guide to take the name "Orin," just as many of you have the same names.

We are part of a larger collective, or multidimensional, consciousness. We do sense ourselves as individuals, even though we are part of a greater whole. You will still feel like an individual as you grow, become one with your soul, and move into multidimensional consciousness. The "I" you call yourself will encompass an even larger identity, just as you now have a larger identity than you did as a child.

There are other guides who feel similar to me and talk about the things I do, for there are many guides who come from my reality or my level of multidimensional reality. I and other guides broadcast on a certain frequency or wave band, and have similar messages of love and peace. Because many of our individual differences are very subtle and are discernible only outside of your normal ability to sense energy, you may not be able to tell the difference between us until you have greatly expanded your consciousness and awareness.

Can You Lose Your Channeling Ability?

ORIN AND DABEN *Channeling is a skill and connection that once made doesn't cease unless you ask it to; however, it may change in form. There may be periods of your life when you stop channeling for short or long periods of time. We have found that most people who elect to stop for various reasons are able to start again when they feel ready.*

Certain conditions will change your direct connection with a guide. People who are going through major health crises may experience temporary suspensions of their verbal connections. In part, this is because it takes a certain level of harmony in your energy bodies to reach us. When people are ill, they may not be able to achieve the harmony necessary to verbally channel. We never withdraw our love and protection; it is only your verbal connection that may be diminished. Once you regain your health, the verbal connection will be as strong as ever.

We only withdraw our verbal connection for your good.

Another condition that can create a temporary suspension of channeling is grief. Those who are in mourning, have lost a loved one, or are grieving for any reason may find that their verbal connections are more difficult, if not impossible, to attain. Grief and sadness are very powerful emotions. Temporary emotions of sadness will not block the connection, but grief is a shock to your entire system and it may take awhile for you to achieve the harmony necessary for a verbal connection. Strong emotions can act like layers of clouds around you, and they make it difficult for us to reach through to you. We will speak to you in your mind when you are grieving, but we will most likely not come all the way into your physical body. We may also send you the friends, events, and information that will act to heal you.

16 GOING OUT TO THE WORLD AS A CHANNEL

Supportive Friends:
One Key to Your Success

SANAYA AND DUANE   It has been important to the development of many well-known channels to keep their channeling initially within a circle of supportive friends. A warm, personal environment is more conducive to awakening and opening people's channeling abilities than a cold, clinical, or judgmental environment. Start by channeling for people who have a basic belief in the process, not for people who you have to convince that channeling is real. You can meet receptive people through new age centers and organizations.

Stepping out in public prematurely can create problems, particularly if you aren't yet confident in your ability to channel. Inexperienced channels can feel other people's doubts and fears so strongly that it often shuts down the connection to their guide. Criticism can be hard to take at first, when you aren't completely sure and confident yourself.

One woman had loved her channeling and her guide up until she gave a reading to a friend who wasn't getting what she wanted from her husband. Duane had clearly seen the guide's presence in the woman's aura when she had channeled during the course. The woman's guide told the friend quite truthfully and compassionately that it was time for her to stop trying to get her husband to act the way she wanted and accept him for who he was. The guide gently and lovingly told the friend that it was time she stopped being a victim and started learning to create what she wanted for herself, because she had the power to create a wonderful, happy life. The friend had responded by telling her that she was sure the channeling was just coming from her personality and not from a guide. Not yet totally confident in her abilities, the woman was so crushed that she stopped channeling. This experience of another's skepticism brought all her own doubts about her channeling to the surface. It took her several months to start again. She was finally able to realize that her friend was threatened by her new role of authority, and wasn't ready to give up the pattern of being a victim. Before channeling she had usually just sympathized with her friend about her "bad" husband. All this had changed after channeling. Her guide was more concerned with helping her friend create a happy, fulfilled life than listening to her complaints. Once she realized why her friend was responding this way, she resumed her channeling. She also realized that her friend gave her a gift by doubting her channeling, for in facing and examining her doubts she became an even stronger and clearer channel.

An attractive, highly paid businesswoman, who had flown in from Boston, had an intense desire to channel, but felt it wouldn't be the sort of thing she could tell her friends about. She brought in a guide at the course and did quite well channeling for other people. When she left, she was fairly confident in her ability to channel. But when she got home, her husband would hardly speak to her because of what he thought of as her foolishness, and her friends looked at her as if she was talking in a foreign language. Some even acted as if they doubted her mental stability when she mentioned she was channeling a guide.

She called us several times to say she was having trouble maintaining her connection with her guide in the face of everyone's doubts. Orin reassured her by telling her that she had chosen to develop belief in herself, even when others didn't support what she was doing. He pointed out that throughout life she had gone on to do many things of which others were critical which had worked out well. He also encouraged her to meet other people who would support her channeling.

A few months later, she called to say she had gone to the local metaphysical bookstore where she had found classes to take, and had met a few friends she could talk to about this new side of her life. Her husband still didn't see any value in channeling, but he wasn't openly hostile any more. She was still very much in the business world, and was finding it a great challenge to continue believing in what she was doing in the face of all the disapproval and apathy that surrounded her. Orin encouraged her to explore whether or not she wanted to remain in the business world, and examine the possibility of fulfilling her lifelong dream, quitting work and writing a book. It was a difficult decision for her. She was worried that she couldn't write, didn't think she could afford to quit work, and thought her husband would strenuously object.

A year later she called again. She had quit her job, and was writing her book. Her channeling had helped her find the courage to move in this direction, and amazing things were happening as she wrote. She had gotten much of the research material she needed that she had thought would be difficult to obtain. Her husband had surprisingly supported her writing and somehow the bills were still getting paid. She was no longer bothered by what others thought, and was enthusiastic and happy with her life. She felt a new trust and confidence in herself. She still had doubts about completing the book, and difficulty believing that she could really have what she wanted, but she knew these would go away with time.

Another problem people encounter is their expectation that after they learn to channel they will be able to channel professionally overnight or that all of their problems will be solved. One young woman had gone through a difficult time just prior to opening to channel. She had gained a lot of weight and broken up with her boyfriend, but she now felt that things were turning around. She still didn't feel a lot of confidence in herself, but was beginning to lose weight and take care of her body. She worked as an office manager and wanted to channel either as a professional, or for friends, and discover her own path and higher purpose. She felt that her current career was only temporary and would end when she found her true spiritual path. She was very enthusiastic about learning to channel and couldn't wait for the connection to her guide, although she was really worried she wouldn't have a guide or that she would have trouble making the connection.

She was so nervous the morning of the course that her stomach hurt. She did well, however, and was very happy with herself. When she channeled, her voice changed, and her guide used gestures that were distinctly different from hers. Most of all she brought through clear, high information. About four months later, she called to say she was having trouble partly because her friends weren't interested or supportive. She had been feeling that her connection to her guide was not as strong as it had been before. She had expected by this time that she would feel total confidence in herself and know exactly what her path was. She had also hoped that she would be out in public channeling professionally.

Orin told her: *"You are still experiencing just a fraction of your guide's true energy. Your physical body could not handle more at this time. In fact, your guide came in a bit more rapidly and took you higher than he originally intended because of your great enthusiasm. He has pulled back a bit to allow your body, emotions, and outer world to catch up. Your guide is transmitting large blocks of data at once, and then waiting awhile for the next transmission, giving you time to assimilate the information and keep the channel open on your own. Do not worry when the waves seem to be gone. It is like the tide going out; it will come back in. Your guide is giving you time now to think for yourself, so you will not grow dependent or think that your wisdom comes just from your channeling.*

"Be patient! Enjoy the process of getting to know your guide. Take time to put your own life in order. The early stages offer you much growth and richness. You are like a child learning to walk,

and you need time to practice and get steady before going out in the world. Later on you will put your work out to the world, but first you will want to develop a strong, solid foundation built on experience and wisdom. Your inner self may need to change a great deal before you are ready to change jobs and take on the responsibility of serving others through channeling professionally. It may take several years before you are ready. True self-confidence cannot be given to you by your guide, for it is a gift you give yourself. Everything you are doing is accelerating your higher path, even if it doesn't seem related. Once you have asserted that you intend to follow your path, everything that happens helps you do so.

"You may also have a picture that being on your path means being well-known, having a lot of people coming to your guide. Achieving higher consciousness is the most important thing you can do to help others, for as you grow, you become a broadcasting station to others. You become a tuning fork and others will begin to experience higher consciousness just by being around you. Many of the great teachers taught by example and by putting their own lives in order. People would report that they felt enlightened just by being near them. As you raise your consciousness, you are on your path. The specific details and form will come later. Everything you desire will come with time.

"Your guide isn't going to tell you what your path is, he's going to help you reach a higher vibration so you can see it for yourself. His main priority now is helping you stabilize and strengthen the higher vibration you have brought through as you connected to the higher realms. He has already helped you think in higher ways, yet you do not recognize it because the changes have been gentle and compatible with your previous direction. Soon your outer world will catch up with the changes in your inner world. The emphasis of change is being shifted from your outer world to the development of your inner life. After you go through this period you will find yourself opening to another level of information from your guide. You may be feeling frustrated. Part of your growth right now is to open your heart, have faith *in yourself and your guide, and learn to trust that you will get what you want. This is part of your opening process and most probably will continue as long as you are evolving."*

The reading helped her let go of her frustration and anxiety and enjoy her channeling more. Once she let go of worrying, the changes that she had been wanting began to occur. She was promoted at work, received a salary increase, took up baseball, and continued to lose weight. She put her channeling aside for awhile, but, six months later, it started coming back into her life and her connection is now strong and stable. A year and a half later, she reports that an opportunity to start her own retail business with a friend is becoming a reality. It isn't what she expected, but she suspects that learning to run her own business might be a step towards becoming a professional channel, teaching her how to serve others, manage her money, and other valuable skills. She says she is learning to trust what comes and let go of trying to make everything happen in a certain way.

Your New Role with Friends

ORIN AND DABEN *Represent your guide and your work with your guide with respect. The confidence and compassion you project through your channeling will determine how others will respond to it. Your presentation of your channeling—as well as your words, attention to detail, and appearance—will tell others about the quality of your work. Take the time to channel carefully, with accuracy and precision, and present your guide in the best possible light. Your integrity, love, and personality are also reflected in the readings. You are your guide's representative on the earth plane.*

When you give readings to people, you will be acting as a life-counselor. Your role will be that of a helper to other people in all aspects of their lives, including spiritual growth. They will look to you more and more as a teacher and healer. Channeling for other people often involves a change of your identity. Your guide will probably speak with more authority and power than you nor-

mally do, so you may be viewed by others as the authority and the person in charge. You will need to get used to speaking with this new level of wisdom. Some people have found that accepting this new role is the most difficult part of channeling for others. With this role come both the opportunity to help others in greater ways and the responsibility for acting with great integrity.

Don't feel you need people to come to you. Simply ask for the people you can best serve, who will truly benefit at a soul level from your work, and you will find them coming to you. You may want to magnetize those people who share similar vibrations and who can thus appreciate what you are doing. Rather than sending your energy out, DRAW IN such people to you. Pretend you are a magnet and are magnetizing to yourself those who can grow and be served by what you have to offer.

> As you channel you radiate more light
> and become more magnetic to people.

You will naturally begin to attract people who are on the same accelerated growth path and can relate to your new interest. You may find that you enjoy being with different people in the future. Old friends who aren't interested in growing may leave your life. You may not enjoy being with people who seem to have no purpose in their lives. You may find opportunities to clean up old issues with friends. You will also find many new friends coming into your life as you are ready.

How to Talk About Channeling with Others

DUANE   Many who have learned to channel find they want to talk about channeling or explain what it is to their friends. Channeling is an experience, and as with any experience it is hard to describe. Channeling is also a part of a reality that has to be individually experienced to have meaning. We have found it best to come from your experience in attempting to explain channeling. Tell your friends what channeling means to you and talk about some of your personal experiences with channeling.

People you talk with about channeling may have responses that range from a very enthusiastic, "that's incredible, I want to know more!" to "that's impossible," or even, "that's dangerous!" Since you'll have found a new sense of friendship with people who have the first response, let your own enthusiasm guide you. You may be surprised or at a loss for words when you encounter people who have the second response, so we'll give you our experiences and Orin's and DaBen's counsel.

First, when you encounter doubt, be understanding, not defensive. Remember that your friends are not the first to question or be in disbelief about this phenomenon of channeling. At one time, you probably questioned it yourself. Attempting to "prove" channeling to those who haven't experienced it or don't believe it is possible will seem to make your realities even more separate. You do not have to prove anything. Your own inner knowingness is your ultimate source of authority, not the thoughts or opinions of others. Remain true to your own integrity, for ultimately all any of us have to offer another is the example of our own lives working. Use your inner truth and your channeling to make your life work. It is also important for you to allow other people to have their truths. Some people would have to reorganize their entire lives to accept these ideas, a frightening prospect for anyone, as you yourself may remember. Remain open, stay in the present, and listen as people around you gain higher levels of consciousness, for as they grow they may seek you out to discuss these ideas with you.

"Proving" that guides exist and that the process of channeling is "valid" presents a number of far-reaching difficulties. We have learned that, in the end, the proof of anything is whatever constitutes proof to the individual. When we accept something as true, we examine and compare the evidence according to our own criteria. If it passes our tests we accept it as proven and base our view of reality or our actions upon it. We accept things in our lives every day as proven without examining the underlying assumptions. Indeed, we couldn't get very much done if we had to spend time and effort to "prove" everything we come in contact with.

In a very real sense our beliefs determine, on an individual basis, what our world is. We accept the existence of atoms without ever having seen them ourselves. We accept information about everything from the conditions on the freeways to news from around the world. We accept it without asking for proof, based on trust that the people providing the information are careful observers and understand the topic well enough to draw accurate conclusions. Often when we actually verify the information, we find that their conclusions or observations differ from ours. Ultimately, our own experiences as individuals mean the most to us.

There are other times when our beliefs, unexamined for too long, don't serve us well. Believing that the earth was flat prevented the discovery of new territory for many, many years. Channeling is one of those areas in which society's beliefs have been too long unexamined, and they are beginning to be re-examined by many people like you. Channeling challenges people to examine their beliefs about the nature of reality and offers great potential for expanding mankind's view of what is possible. It brings people in contact with ideas that are on the frontiers of what mankind can "prove" at this point in its evolution. These ideas determine how we view ourselves and form the basis of our philosophy, religion, and science. Changes in these ideas have the power to truly bring about paradigm shifts for mankind. Channeling immediately opens for transformation and transcendence our frameworks of thought on life after death, intelligent life in the universe, the nature of matter, and the nature of biological systems. This seems to be just a beginning of the openings for change that could be brought about through channeling.

Science is often used as the test of whether something is "real." In part, this is due to a trust that scientists have in their colleagues' findings. They rarely question more than the conclusions drawn from such data, relying on the honesty and integrity of their fellow scientists in relaying accurate information. This is particularly true if the conclusions fit their own or society's accepted views. These conclusions become underlying, and often hidden, assumptions on which other scientists base their studies. Later it is sometimes found that the underlying assumptions were wrong. Anyone familiar with the history of science has seen that new theories, which are later shown to be true and greatly change our view of the world, have often been rejected by established science for years without real examinations of the issues involved.

Something fascinating occurs when scientists look at channeling. Channeling is a part of what science has broadly called "paranormal phenomena." The word "paranormal" itself is a problem. Paranormal is generally used to describe any phenomena that are outside normal reality. Scientists are attempting to define the nature of reality. Since the label paranormal implies that something is not a part of normal reality, paranormal phenomena are clearly at odds with the scientist's logic from the beginning. This seems to be reflected in the typical scientist's response that the paranormal either does not happen or it does happen, but, since it can't be easily explained, for sanity's sake it should be ignored. Both of these are interesting responses from people whose training promotes exploration, and hopefully eventual explanation of the unexplained.

In exploring new areas we encounter the unknown. Many of us respond to the unknown with apprehension. Each individual has his or her areas of fear/excitement; each society has its areas of fear/excitement. There are sometimes social pressures against bringing these unexplained areas to the attention of the public. However, as the unknown becomes known, fears are overcome and often the new ideas are embraced enthusiastically.

When I began my explorations of the New Age, I was quite firmly a skeptic. After several individually distinct experiences and a wealth of insights on self-exploration over several years, however, the weight of the evidence was too large to ignore and my beliefs began to shift. I began to realize that although my experiences could not be scientifically explained or proven, they were valuable and, surprisingly, consistent and reliable enough to use. In short, they produced results.

Given the difficulties in proving experiential phenomena, perhaps it is most important to remember the observable fact that channeling, as we have defined it, is making a positive and significant contribution to people in their real-world and spiritual activities. The channels we have observed are productive; in fact, a number are prestigious members of society. Many were prosperous and successful before they consciously undertook channeling and they use channeling in many ways, as their stories indicate. People became more successful after they began channeling, and they put their lives into greater order.

As my scientist side looks at channeling now, although I "know" a lot about it, I still can't prove it scientifically. There is a wealth of circumstantial and indirect evidence, enough to prove to me that something is happening, something that we cannot explain from our present perspective of reality. I can observe that it produces positive results on a consistent basis. I have stopped trying to "prove" channeling is real, and now use a more business-oriented approach: "If it works, use it."

Going Public

SANAYA AND DUANE   Some of you will be ready sooner than others to go public with your channeling. Listen to your own feelings about this and don't feel that you must offer your readings to others prematurely. People who go out in a big way quickly, often have had prior experience as counselors or healers, and are already experienced at talking to others and helping them.

One woman, Julie, who had done bodywork and professional counseling, was asked to give a talk at a local women's college. As a professional counselor, she had given talks on topics of her choosing every year to a group of what she had thought were fairly conservative women. She had just begun channeling a month before, and her guide urged her to share her many recent experiences with channeling. At first she wouldn't even consider doing this because she didn't want to create resistance or be told she was way out on a limb. She told her guide, "No," and planned a standard speech. At the last minute, sitting in front of the room, a shift took place inside her. She decided to take a risk and trust her guide, and tell the women about her channeling. The response was amazing. The women were fascinated and wanted to learn all they could. Far from being cold or skeptical, they loved the topic. Many of them began to talk about experiences they had been having that they had kept secret because they were afraid others would laugh at them. She said the closeness and warmth that resulted went beyond anything she had experienced before.

With this response as encouragement, Julie decided to hold monthly meetings at her home and channel her guide, Jason, for her clients. Her guide picked subjects every week and channeled on them for a group of people. From these channelings she started writing a book, while more and more people continued to come. Her private practice became so large she had to find ways to handle all the people who wanted to see her. Studying with Duane, she also learned to see clairvoyantly. She worked with us and has assisted many people in the Opening to Channel course, helping them to harmonize their energies.

Julie was ready to put her channeling out to the public because of all the prior years of experience she had counseling and leading classes. Honor whatever pace is comfortable for you; be patient. Your work with your guide will unfold at its natural speed.

Your Relationship
to Other Channels

ORIN AND DABEN *There are many of you opening to channel, and it is important to support and encourage others in their openings. Each one of you has a valuable contribution to make. As you open to channeling, you become part of the larger community of all other people who are channeling. As all of you think and act in new ways, you are spreading higher, more loving thoughtforms throughout the world. Form follows thought. Real changes will happen on earth as more and more of you open and refine your channel to higher dimensions and bring that increased light through to your daily lives. In the higher realms, many things are accomplished by working together with a group of like-minded people. As more of you open, you form a grid-work of light around the planet, creating a higher potential for mankind. It is through working together, supporting, and empowering each other that each one of you will be propelled even further in whatever direction you are going.*

Celebrate each other's successes— hold a positive, high vision for others.

People may ask you what you think of other people's guides. There are many perspectives to every issue. Part of your growth will be to find the highest perspective you can on any issue in your life. When someone asks about a guide, rather than judge the guide to be all good or all bad, unless you have a very strong opinion one way or another, ask, "What particular information do you want my or my guide's opinion on?" Then respond by commenting on that information. If you are hearing the information secondhand, attempt to learn exactly what the guide said. Even the highest guides will occasionally say things you don't know about, or don't agree with, or have a different perspective on. This simply means you are following your own experience, as you should, not that the guide is wrong. Using this approach will help keep you from feeling you must "judge" other guides in the right or wrong framework, and instead let you respond with you or your guide's perspective on the issue.

Often people feel that there is no point in putting out their work, writing their books, or teaching their classes, because so many other people are already doing similar things. Instead, we suggest that every person who is getting his or her work out is making it that much easier for you to get your work out. There is a great plan of mankind's evolution, and each of you has a special part in it. One person alone couldn't possibly create the shift to higher consciousness that is occurring. Each one of you has a valuable contribution.

Don't let the numbers of other people doing what appear to be the same things you want to do stop you. There is always room for another good book. Even if several books have been written on a topic, write your book anyway if you have the urge to do so. Your message, the way you say it, and the energy in your words, will reach a different group of people than another author's books. If you find that someone is teaching a subject similar to what you want to teach, teach your class anyway. It will carry your energy, reach the people who need your teaching, and open them up in a unique way. There are more than enough interested people for every one of you to have your classes full, your books bought, and abundant support of your services and products.

To bring through a new thoughtform, it is necessary for many people from all walks of life, in many different fields, to put out similar messages. The more times people come across a certain idea, particularly if it is said in different ways by different people, the more real that idea will become for them. As it becomes more real, a shift in consciousness is created for many other people. Go for it, and get your work out to the world if that is your true desire.

17 CHANNELING— THE TIME IS NOW

Channeling in the Past

SANAYA AND DUANE   Now is not the first time that people have been interested in connecting with entities from other planes. The following gives you some basic information about a few well-known channels and a sketch of the highlights in the recent history of channeling. There are many excellent channels today, and we encourage you to follow your interests as you explore their books, classes, and audio and video tapes as a way to learn more about channeling and guides. In the past, people who connected with spirits called themselves "mediums." Those who went into trance to bring through connections to spirits called themselves "trance mediums." This description is currently being replaced by the word "channel."

Around the middle of the nineteenth century there was enormous public interest in the phenomenon of spirit communication. Table rappings, telekinesis (the movement of objects by an invisible force), materializations (the temporary and visible appearances of faces, eyes, heads, or full bodies of spirits), levitation (the lifting of objects by an invisible force), and many other unexplainable happenings were taking place. Communication with spirits became such a popular topic that it was reported in 1862 that Nettie Colburn, a powerful young trance medium, visited the White House and gave a trance reading to President Abraham Lincoln on the eve of his Antislavery Proclamation.

John Fox and the Fox sisters are credited with activating the tremendous interest in the world of spirits and starting the Spiritualist Movement in the mid-1800s. This apparently began when they moved into a house and heard constant rappings, knocks, and noises. One night, trying to find relief from the noises, Mrs. Fox asked if there was a presence; if so, would it rap twice for yes and once for no. Communication was immediately established with a spirit. Through yes and no rappings, he was found to be a thirty-one-year-old male former tenant of the house, who claimed that he had been murdered and that his body was in the cellar. Within several weeks hundreds of people were coming to hear the rappings. A skeleton was found in the cellar exactly where he said it would be. Mrs. Fox had three daughters, who became known as the Fox sisters. Wherever they went, rappings began to appear, and the daughters became mediums and did many public sittings. After they became mediums, many well-known people attended the sessions they held, and the Fox sisters became topics of public interest. It is interesting to note that many who came to watch the Fox sisters became mediums themselves. It seems that just being around them triggered openings in others.

Many other mediums, as they were then called, came to public attention. Daniel Douglas Home was considered one of the greatest physical mediums, for he could produce levitations, music without instruments, and all manner of telekinetic manifestations. Phantom hands could be seen on occasion, as well as other visible manifestations of spirits. He was studied by some of the leading scientists of the day, several of whom almost lost their reputations and positions because of their subsequent written statements verifying the reality of those phenomena. Several of these scientists later became mediums themselves. Home also had the ability to pass on his special talents to the people around him, provided they had faith. In one instance he passed on his immunity to fire by putting a red hot coal into the hand of a woman while he was holding her hand. She reported it felt cold, like marble. Seconds later, without his help, she went to touch it and withdrew immediately, saying that it burned her.

Rev. Stainton Moses was another well-known medium who produced many documented physical manifestations, such as the levitation of tables. He was conscious as he channeled the inspirational writings of his guide and was very concerned that his thoughts not influence the automatic writing. He wrote: "It is an interesting subject for speculation whether my own thoughts entered into the subject matter of the communications. I took extraordinary pains to prevent any such admixture. At first the writing was slow, and it was necessary for me to follow it with my eye, but even then the thoughts were not my thoughts. Very soon the messages assumed a character of which I had no doubt whatever that the thought was opposed to my own. But I cultivated the power of occupying my mind with other things during the time that the writing was going on." Stainton Moses channeled high, inspirational guidance and contributed much to the credibility of spirit guidance. He lost his ability to bring through the channelings from time to time due to a recurring illness.

Andrew Jackson Davis made a large impact on spiritualism with his book *Principles of Nature, Her Divine Revelations.* One night he wandered out of his bed, in a semi-trance, and woke up the next day 40 miles away, in the mountains. He said he met two philosophers, long since deceased, who assisted him in achieving a state of inner illumination. He then spent 15 months dictating this major work covering a wide array of topics. It contained startling information, vast in scope, much of which was later proven true by scientific means. For instance, the writings revealed things he could not have known, such as the statement that there were nine planets, at a time when there were thought to be seven with the possibility of an eighth only suspected.

Mrs. Piper was another well-known medium of the time and perhaps one of the most tested. She started channeling when she was twenty-two, bringing through one guide for eight years before another came in. Her guides were able to give people many accurate details of their pasts, things she could not have possibly known, although she seemed to have trouble giving dates and specific information under test conditions. It is of note that even the most well-known channels found it difficult to give specifics such as names or dates when tested, but they were able to give detailed information about what their guide felt was important or contributed to people's lives and spiritual growth.

Mrs. Piper was tested by a Dr. Hodgson, who became like a Sherlock Holmes to the psychic world, testing and verifying the accuracy of mediums. He had her followed day and night to make sure she did not secretly obtain information about people. She did readings from behind a curtain so she couldn't see the people, who were identified to her only as Smith. Again and again her detailed information about people was documented and the accuracy verified. Eventually, her earlier guides left and later in life she brought in high guidance from a source which identified itself as the Imperator Group. It is notable that as she moved to higher and higher guides, the process of getting into trance, which had been difficult for her before, became a quiet, peaceful, and easy transition.

Around the same time, Alan Kardec, a Frenchman, produced many books on spirit communications, including *The Book of Mediums and Spirit Guides,* both of which are still in print today. If you would like to read more about the early history of channeling, a book called *An Encyclopaedia of Psychic Science,* written by Nandor Fodor in 1934 and recently updated, may be of value to you.

One of the most influential and controversial mediums of the times was Madame Helene Blavatsky, known as HPB. Born in 1831 in the Ukraine, she traveled to such places as England, Canada, India, and Greece, and unusual physical phenomena accompanied her wherever she went. She was joined by Henry Olcott, and together they formed the Theosophical Society. Her first book, *Isis Unveiled,* a classic even today, discusses the revival of ancient religions and identifies them as the underlying sources of the religions of her day. She felt that she was inspired and working with a secret hierarchy of Himalayan Masters, including the Masters Morya, Kut Humi, and the Tibetan Master Djwhal Khul. These Masters sent many letters to her friend, A. P. Sinnett, in India, as well as several others, that became known as the Mahatma letters. The letters would arrive by dropping from the ceiling, or appearing on plates or in pockets. There was much controversy about whether or not these Masters really existed, and whether she, not they, wrote the letters. Later in life, she said she took dictation from these Far Eastern Masters for her major book, *Secret Doctrines.* In this book it is asserted that all religions and systems of occult belief come from a single source. The source is believed to be hidden in a secret place and revealed only in cryptic, arcane symbols.

The highly regarded Theosophical Society is still in existence today, and HPB has had a very influential role in the Western belief in the Great Masters. Her work was carried on by Annie Besant and Charles Leadbeater, who produced books in the early 1900s on many esoteric topics, including Thoughtforms, Clairvoyant Sight, Karma, the Chakras, Spirit Guides, and many more.

In 1919 a very dedicated young woman named Alice Bailey began receiving information from the Tibetan Master Djwhal Khul and took daily dictation from him, producing a whole series of books containing much valuable esoteric information. She founded her own Theosophical Association, which she renamed The Arcane School in 1923. She set up a whole series of organizations, including Triangles, a worldwide meditative network; the Lucis Trust; and the Lucis Press to publish her books. The books describe the path of an initiate, the hierarchy of masters and the White Brotherhood, and the initiations one experiences as one moves toward becoming a master. World service is stressed. The term "New Age" was derived from her writings.

After the first world war, a national depression, and an emphasis on technology and science, the public's earlier enthusiasm waned and spiritualism ceased to be front-page news. Logical, left-brain thinking came into dominance with a wave of scientific inventions and new technology.

Edgar Cayce, called the "sleeping prophet," was responsible for creating renewed national interest in the phenomenon of channeling in the mid-twentieth century. When he was hypnotized, he could produce astonishing information, including medical cures for people thousands of miles away. He gave profound philosophical discussions on various topics which are contained in many books about his works and life. He was dedicated to serving mankind, and the A.R.E. Foundation is carrying on his important work today. His healing formulas and channeled information are on file and still available to the public from the foundation's headquarters in Virginia Beach, Virginia.

Jane Roberts has recently awakened many to the value of quality channeled information. Starting in the 1960s, she and her guide, Seth, channeled volumes of information and philosophical discussions about a variety of topics. Her books are well-written, informative, and positive about many metaphysical and esoteric topics. They empower the individual to believe in himself and to accept that each person has the power within to create whatever he desires. One of her most popular books, *The Nature of Personal Reality,* explains the nature of reality and emphasizes our ability to change outcomes by changing our beliefs. Her books set a standard of quality and integrity for channeled information and opened many people to the possibility of guides, as well as inspiring many people to want to channel themselves.

It is noteworthy that fewer and fewer mediums are able to produce physical phenomena such as materializations of the guides and table rappings. When asked about this, Orin and DaBen told us that these manifestations had been necessary in earlier days to awaken mankind to its ability to connect with other planes of reality and to help establish a belief in guides and life beyond death. These vivid, scientifically verifiable, and photographically documented phenomena were needed to awaken people and set the stage for mankind's next level of development in this area. Enough people now believe in channeling that dramatic events are no longer as necessary as they were before. Some well-known channels today who are dramatic in the presentations of their guides have volunteered to be this way to help people believe guides are real. It takes much energy from the guides to create these phenomena, and now this same energy is being used to reach more and more people. Orin and DaBen tell us that conscious channeling is the next stage in mankind's abilities to channel.

Channeling—The Time Is Now for Mankind

ORIN AND DABEN *More and more people are awakening to their connections with the universal mind and to their higher selves. They are becoming aware of the higher realms of the universe. Throughout recorded history there have always been people in contact with worlds beyond the known universe. They have been called by various names: shamans, medicine men and women, seers, prophets, oracles, psychics, mediums, channels, and healers. However, it has only been in the last 150 years that a significant number of people have been able to reach beyond the earth plane and bring through guidance from higher realms. The energy that enables them to reach these higher realms has intensified in the last fifty years, as demonstrated by the wave of scientific and technological inventions.*

*You have the ability to see
and connect with realities beyond
the visible and known universe.*

Many high souls are choosing to incarnate at this time; their numbers have increased during the last sixty years and are still continuing to increase. As more and more people believe in channeling and in the intuitive faculty, there will be an increase in those who are open to these levels and who are born with psychic, telepathic, and extrasensory abilities.

More and more people will be
opening to channel.

This is a time in which people who put their energies into growing spiritually will be abundantly rewarded. They will be able to
evolve rapidly because the earth is energized right now. They can
acquire the ability to reach new levels of awareness and bring
through information and data from the higher realms consciously
and controllably. The ability to explore the self as it exists in other
dimensions and mediums is more possible than ever before.
More people than ever possess the ability to channel, explore
alternate and probable futures, move into new understandings
and concepts of time, control the mind and unconscious, and
tap into the powers of their superconscious selves. As more people travel into other dimensions and higher realms, a doorway
is created for many more who would not have been able to make
such journeys before.

It is not coincidental that all of this is happening now. There
are many forces that are affecting mankind. Changes are occurring in dimensions beyond the earth; doorways are being created
to other planes of reality that have never before been accessible
to people. Two dimensions are intersecting and moving together
in such a way that anyone who desires to can access higher
dimensions that were once only easily reached by a few people
with exceptional sensitivity. While these changes are felt more
by those who are in contact with their spiritual selves, they affect everyone to some degree.

There is a continuing step-up in the vibration of the earth. It
will be perceived as an acceleration by some. The nature of time
is changing; you are moving from linear time to a more intuitive
sense of time. Gravity is altering slightly and changes are occurring in the electromagnetic frequencies of the earth.

For the last 150 years you have been developing new perceptions called "extrasensory." These extrasensory perceptions include precognition (the ability to know the future), telepathy
(thought transference), and clairvoyance (the ability to see

energies that are normally invisible, possibly occurring on another plane of existence altogether). These faculties are developing because of the activation of your spiritual centers and the earth changes. These earth changes will affect many people and will definitely change the potential and direction of your collective future.

Telepathy enables you to explore unseen worlds. All of you have more telepathic ability than you imagine. Telepathy is the ability to receive thought-impulses from other people, and the ability to transfer thoughts from one dimension or reality to another. As your telepathic ability evolves, you develop a vehicle to take you to places faster and more effectively than airplanes or cars. Telepathy gives you the ability to travel to places that are not accessible through any other means.

Your eyes can only see the spectrum of the rainbow, and you often forget that there are many electromagnetic frequencies, such as infrared and ultraviolet frequencies that are just outside of the range you detect with your eyes. Some of you are developing the ability to sense subtle frequencies beyond the range of your normal senses. It is in these frequencies that you become aware of guides and of the realms where other living entities such as ourselves exist. Your increasing telepathic awareness gives you the ability to communicate with other life forms such as plants and crystals, and beings from other realms, as you fine-tune your awareness.

The belief in the ability to reach these unseen though nonetheless real dimensions is not yet commonplace, but there is increasing worldwide belief in the possibility of the existence of dimensions beyond the earth itself, as well as a belief in life beyond death. The willingness to be open to the possibility of spirit guides has increased greatly, and the enthusiasm and excitement that is prevalent today around channeling and spirit guides makes it much easier for those who have the desire to connect consciously with their guides. There is more trust in the information brought in through extrasensory awareness than in the past.

The golden age of man is coming.

The energies hitting the earth right now will energize and ac-tivate whatever you are focusing on. For those of you who are sensitive and already focusing on your spiritual path, these new energies will make things work out better than ever before. Doors will open; your relationships will improve. You may find yourself looking inward, finding the answers you've been searching for. You may go through some temporarily difficult times as you let go of the old and receive the new. Many of you have already gone through this period of adjustment. On the other side of it is a better life, filled with more abundance, love, and success. Ap-preciate your lessons now as they come, and know that they are preparing you to handle a higher vibration.

You may still see others in pain or difficulty. You may still read of disturbing world events. The challenge as you reach these higher realms is to remember that your balance will now be com-ing from a connection to the higher realms, rather than to other people. You will be able to provide balance and stability for others as you make this connection. It is important to help those who you see are having difficulty adjusting to the new vibrations, rather than getting caught up in their fears. As you open your channel, you will be the one holding the light, bringing positive encouragement and direction to others. It is a time of great op-portunity. Some of mankind's greatest music, art, writing, and cultural expressions are yet to come, and will be produced under the influence of this higher vibration.

Find Your Time to Begin

SANAYA AND DUANE It has been two years now since Orin and DaBen first suggested we teach channeling. We have watched hundreds of people gain mastery over their lives as they con-nected with their guides or source selves, awakening to their in-ner teachers and discovering their abilities to transform them-selves and others. We have watched people succeed with their lives, become happier, more prosperous, and discover their life purpose through channeling. Our own experiences with channeling have greatly enriched our lives. We have found in Orin and DaBen constant sources of love, guidance, and growth.

According to our experience and that of others, channeling IS a skill that can be learned. Guides do come to people when they request the connection. Orin and DaBen were right. We have experienced deep satisfaction in watching and assisting people in opening to channel. It is possible for people to gain enlightenment, to achieve the higher consciousness they desire. Channeling is one of the doorways, and we are grateful for the opportunity to offer it to you.

Before you put this book down, decide when you want to open to channel and connect with your guide. Close your eyes, sit quietly, and ask your higher self to give you a date by which you could start. It might be today or a year from now. Once you have a date in mind, ask yourself if you intend to channel by then. Is it too soon, or does it give you more time than you need to be ready? Keep picturing dates until you have one that feels best. Open your eyes and mark this date on a calendar, then let it go. Your higher self will now begin to bring about all the circumstances, coincidences, growth opportunities, and events needed to make this happen. As you follow and act on your inner messages, whatever you do will be preparing you to open to channel.

COMPANION BOOKS
BY ORIN AND DABEN

BOOK I OF THE EARTH LIFE SERIES

Living with Joy
Keys to Personal Power and Spiritual Transformation
This book teaches you how to love and nurture yourself, live in higher purpose, and discover your life purpose. You will learn how to radiate love; be compassionate, tolerant, and forgiving; feel inner peace; take a quantum leap; gain clarity; open to new things; trust your inner guidance; change negatives into positives; and open to receive. You will learn to raise your vibration by increasing your ability to love; have more self-esteem; and create harmony, clarity, and peace around you. You can live with joy rather than struggle.

BOOK II OF THE EARTH LIFE SERIES

Personal Power Through Awareness
A Guidebook for Sensitive People
This is an accelerated, step-by-step course in sensing energy. Using these easy-to-follow processes, thousands have learned to create immediate and profound changes in their relationships, self-image, and ablity to love and be loved. You need no longer be affected by other people's moods or negativity. You can recognize when you have taken on other people's energies and easily release them. You can learn to stay centered and balanced, know who you are, increase the positive energy around you, and help and heal others. Your sensitivity is a gift. Learn to use it to send and receive tele-pathic messages, increase your intuitive abilities, and open to higher guidance. You can leave the denser energies, where things are often painful, and live in the higher energies where you can feel more loving, calm, focused, and positive.

Spiritual Growth
Being Your Higher Self

Spiritual Growth teaches you how to BE your Higher Self in your everyday life, create a vision of your higher purpose, and manifest what you want rapidly and easily. If you want to explore channeling your Higher Self, this book will assist you in learning to do so. You will learn to work with light for healing and growth, connect with the Universal Mind for enhanced creativity, and link with the Higher Will to carry out your higher purpose.You will learn to lift the veils of illusion, see truth, expand and contract time, raise your vibration, achieve higher states of consciousness, open your heart, and know yourself in new, more loving ways. *Spiritual Growth* teaches you to have more satisfying relationships with others by using the skills of non-attachment, right use of will, being transparent to others' energies, and communicating as your Higher Self. You will learn to become a source of light and to grow through world service. This book offers the next step in spiritual growth for you who want to know more about who you are, why you are here, and what you came to do. You can align with the higher energies that are coming into the earth plane and use them to create the best life you can imagine for yourself. These easy-to-learn processes have helped thousands take a quantum leap, accelerate their spiritual growth, and live their lives with more joy, harmony, peace, and love.

Creating Money
Keys to Abundance

By Sanaya Roman and Duane Packer
This step-by-step guide to creating money and abundance was given to Sanaya and Duane by their guides Orin and DaBen. Thousands have manifested prosperity and created their life's work using the simple processes contained in this book. Learn the spiritual laws of abundance, advanced manifesting techniques, and how to discover and draw to yourself your life's work. Learn about magnetism and how to use your magnetic will to draw to you what

you want effortlessly, including the people you can serve and assist and the tools you need to carry out your life's work. Develop unlimited thinking, listen to your inner guidance, and transform your beliefs. Create money as a source of light for yourself and others. You can work with energy to easily create what you want and tap into the unlimited abundance of the universe.

About the Opening to Channel Courses:

If you have read the *Opening to Channel* book and would like further assistance in channeling, we suggest you work with our Opening to Channel tape album (C100 on the next page). These tapes contain the processes used in this book and our Opening to Channel courses. Many people who have wanted more direct contact with Orin and DaBen to assist them in channeling have used these tapes to learn to channel. You can also share these tapes with friends and clients to conduct your own courses. We are no longer teaching the Opening to Channel courses as described in the book. If you have used the processes in the book and tried the Opening to Channel tapes and would like further assistance, our Opening to Channel course assistants are offering their own classes with formats similar to the classes described in the book. They are also available to travel to teach groups or work with you individually. For more information write our office: LuminEssence Creations, P.O. Box 19117, Oakland, CA 94619.

Additional Resources by Orin and DaBen

Opening to Channel: Seminar on tape by Orin and DaBen
These tapes are a wonderful companion to the *Opening to Channel* book. Orin and DaBen will join their energy with yours to assist you in meeting your guide and learning to channel. Orin and DaBen will lead you through each step of channeling, including relaxation, concentration, sensing life-force energy, journeying to mentally meet your guide, trance postures, a guided journey to verbally channel your guide, (including many questions to ask your guide) six trance inductions, and guided meditations to give yourself a reading, view the future, and give readings to other people. 4 tapes with over 16 processes in an attractive vinyl album. *C100 $49.95***

Channeling Skills Seminar on tape – recorded live
This audio cassette channeling course will teach you how to use your connection to your guide to channel on your and others' past-lives; emotional, mental, and physical energy bodies; and chakras. You will explore mind-linking and future traveling through the centuries to open your visionary abilities. Includes ways to open your throat center to bring through more fully the energy, wisdom, and expressions of your guide. Sanaya and Duane talk about channeling and how to break through to new levels, become a clearer channel, and reach a deeper trance state. 4 tapes in attractive vinyl album. *W007 $49.95***

Improve Your Channeling Seminar on tape – recorded live
This audio cassette course is for you who already have a verbal connection to your guide and want to learn to channel new information and strengthen your connection to your guide. Use this to learn how to get into a deeper trance, become a clearer channel, identify core beliefs, and channel while standing. You will learn to channel information on your and others' life purposes, parental programming, relationship patterns, higher purposes of a relationship, your life purpose, and the higher purpose of your job or daily activities. This course also contains talks by Sanaya and Duane about commonly asked questions: how you can gain more confidence in your channeling, let go of doubts, bring through new levels of information, and more. Four tapes in a vinyl album. *W006 $49.95***

Meeting Your Spirit Guide. A beginning journey to sense, see, or hear your guide. A preparatory tape for those who are exploring their readiness to channel. *014 $9.98*

Crystal for channeling: Orin and DaBen have charged a beautiful 1–2" quartz crystal with their energy. Hold it as you channel or to tune into the life-force energy of a crystal. *CRY07 $7.95*

*** Free tape offer does not apply to albums.*

More From Orin

Audio Cassette Tapes

"I offer these guided meditations to you who want to use and live the principles in this book. Working with guided meditations, where your mind is in a relaxed, open state is one of the most powerful ways known to create rapid, profound, and lasting changes in your life. Release subconscious programs that aren't bringing you what you want, and replace them with higher ones. Create immediate results in your life and open to your greater potential as you listen to these guided meditations." – *Orin*

Spiritual Growth: Volume I – Raising Your Vibration

Contains stereo sound frequencies for right/left brain wave synchronization and theta level deep meditation. Guided meditations for: Choosing Your Reality, Raising Your Vibration, Expanding and Contracting Time, Accelerating Your Growth, Right Use of Will, Lifting the Veils of Illusion, Becoming Transparent, and Calming Your Emotions. 4 tapes, 8 processes in cassette album. Beautiful New Age music by Michael Hammer. (SG101) $59.95 ** *(Tapes not sold separately.)*

Spiritual Growth: Volume II – Being Your Higher Self

Contains stereo sound frequencies for right/left brain wave synchronization and theta level deep meditation. Guided meditations for: Connecting with the Universal Mind, Linking with the Higher Will, Being Your Higher Self, Creating with Light, Seeing the Bigger Picture, Non-Attachment, Allowing Your Higher Good, Opening Awareness of the Inner Planes. 4 tapes, 8 processes in cassette album. Music by Michael Hammer. (SG102) $59.95 ** *(Tapes not sold separately.)*

**Buy both Volumes I and II (SG101 and SG102) at the same time for $99.95 and save $19.95. Specify SG103. *(Free tape offer does not apply.)*

Transformation: Evolving Your Personality

These meditations assist you in handling the challenges – such as blockages, doubts, mood swings, old issues coming up, overstimulation, etc. – that come from being on an accelerated path of spiritual growth. Meditations include: Self-Appreciation; Honoring Your Path of Awakening; Focusing Inward: Hearing Your Soul's Voice; Focusing Upward: Hearing the Voice of the Masters and Guides; Reparenting Yourself: Changing the Past; Creating the Future with Light; Beyond Intellect: Opening Your Higher Mind; Journey to the Temple of the Masters to reprogram at cellular, release limitations, old beliefs, blockages, and more. 8 processes, 4 two-sided tapes in album. (SG200) $49.95 *(Contains theta stereo sound frequencies.)*

Becoming a Writer

Four meditations by Orin: I Am a Writer; Manifesting Your Writing; Loving to Write; Connecting with Your Audience. Powerful processes given to Sanaya by Orin to help get their books out to the world. 2 tapes in album. SI016 $29.95 *(Contains alpha to theta stereo sound frequencies.)*

Additional Resources

Guided Meditations by Orin

Spiritual Growth Affirmations Side 1, Guided Journey Side 2. Based on
   principles in book (SG100)
Living With Joy Affirmations and Guided Journey (L100)
Personal Power Through Awareness Affirmations, Guided Journey (P100)
Being Your Higher Self (SI040)
Opening Your Chakras by Orin and DaBen (016)
Who Am I? (017)
Self-Love (L102)
Radiating Unconditional Love (P103)
Opening Spiritually (SG002)
I Am Lovable (SI105)
Traveling into Probable Realities (SI018)
Telepathy–Sensing Energy (015)
Feeling Inner Peace (L101)
For Self-Employed People: Attracting Clients, Business & Money (SI037)
Staying In Your Center (SG003)
Unlimited Thinking (SI108)
Developing Intuition (010)
Discovering Your Life Purpose (L104)
Developing Compassion/Forgiveness (SI104)
The Universe is Perfect, Stop Efforting (SG004)
Opening Up Your Psychic Abilities (013)
Moving Into Higher Consciousness (SI012)
Past-Life Regression (SI043)
Creating Your Perfect Day (SI101)
Lucid Dreaming–Interpreting, Remembering Dreams (SI024)
Opening Creativity (SI046)
Opening to Receive (L106)
Clearing Blockages (SI057)
Taking a Quantum Leap (L103)
Attracting Your Soul-Mate (RE002)
Attunement With Your Crystal by Orin and DaBen (OD001) $12.50

All tapes listed above are $9.98 each unless otherwise indicated. Both sides
of most tapes contain the same meditation. One side has theta or alpha
sound frequency inputs. Include postage as per order form; CA residents
add sales tax. Music by Michael Hammer.

To receive a FREE SUBSCRIPTION to our newsletter with information from
Orin and DaBen on current earth changes, articles of interest, tape programs, and seminars by Orin and DaBen write: LuminEssence Productions,
P.O. Box 19117, Oakland, CA 94619; or call (415) 635-1246. Be sure to
include your name, address and phone number.

Manifesting and Abundance
Creating Money: Keys to Abundance

To increase your prosperity consciousness, Orin has made these Creating Money audio cassette tapes. These tapes are guided meditations that will assist you in reprogramming your subconscious to increase your abundance potential. The tapes in this series are:

Magnetizing Yourself (SI010)
Clearing Beliefs and Old Programs (SI071)
Releasing Doubts and Fears (SI075)
Linking with Your Soul and the Guides (SI076)
Aura Clearing, Energy, and Lightwork (SI073)
Subpersonality Journey: Awakening Your Prosperity Self (SI074)
Success: Releasing Fears of Success, Failure, Going for It! (SI070)
Abundance: Creating Plenty in EVERY Area of Your Life (SI072)

All tapes are $9.98 each. A complete set of all 8 processes as listed above is available in the Creating Money album (M100) for $49.95. The set contains 4 two-sided tapes packaged in a convenient cassette album. Please add postage and tax as per order form. *(Free tape offer does not apply to M100)* (Contains theta sound frequencies and music by Michael Hammer.)

Becoming a World Server: Discovering Your Life Purpose

Discover your life purpose and make it a reality. Journeys by Orin include: The Awakening: What Am I Here to Do?; Sounding Your Note; Expanding Your Vision; Meeting Your Spiritual Community; Calling to You Those You Can Serve; Navigating the Flow; Being a Source of Light; Becoming a World Server. You will work with your Higher Self and the Masters to awaken to your true path; join with the world plan; see the bigger picture of your work; create your ideal job; draw clients, business, students, and opportunities to you; know you are on the right path; see yourself as a leader; call on the assistance that is available from the higher realms; and journey to the Temple of the Masters to energize your work. Set of four two-sided tapes (8 guided meditations) in attractive vinyl album with alpha to theta sound frequency inputs. Music by Michael Hammer. (M200) $49.95 *(Individual tapes not sold separately.)*

Abundance Crystal: Clear quartz crystal charged by Orin to assist you in creating abundance as you hold it. Approximately 1-1/2" – 2". (CRY01) $7.95

Abundance Affirmation Cards: Affirmations from the book *Creating Money*. 112 Affirmations on quality blue-linen calling cards, shrink-wrapped in box. Pull one for your daily abundance affirmation. (CMA) $9.95

Abundance Affirmations Audio Cassette tape by Orin: Side 1 contains the affirmations from the book, Creating Money. Side 2 contains powerful magnetizing techniques to draw to yourself money, small and large objects, and more. (M001) $9.98

Crystals Charged by Orin and DaBen

Orin has personally held and charged each crystal with certain energies to assist you with your spiritual growth. As you hold them, they will help amplify your own energy.

Amethyst crystal: Orin has added some of the higher frequencies of his dimensions to this amethyst cristal to assist you in being your Higher Self. (CRY03) $7.95

Citrine crystal: Hold this as you reprogram and add light at a cellular level and release old patterns. (CRY02) $7.95

Clear Quartz: Orin has charged these 1-1/2"–2" crystals to assist you in exploring the higher dimensions. Can enhance telepathic sending and receiving from guides and masters. (CRY05) $7.95

Books

Living with Joy, by Sanaya Roman, channel for Orin. Keys to Personal Power and Spiritual Transformation. Book I of the Earth Life Series. (H J Kramer Inc, 1986, 216 pages) (LWJ) $10.95

Personal Power Through Awareness, by Sanaya Roman, channel for Orin. A Guidebook for Sensitive People. Book II of the Earth Life Series. (H J Kramer Inc, 1989, 216 pages) (PPTA) $10.95

Spiritual Growth: Being Your Higher Self by Sanaya Roman, channel for Orin. Book III of the Earth Life Series. (H J Kramer Inc, 1989, 252 pages) (SG) $10.95

Creating Money: Keys to Abundance, by Sanaya Roman and Duane Packer, channels for Orin and DaBen. (H J Kramer Inc, 1988, 288 pages) (CM) $12.95

Seminars and Courses

Orin and DaBen give several weekend seminars and intensives throughout the year. Seminars include meditations, energy work, and channeling by Orin and DaBen. To receive a FREE SUBSCRIPTION to our newsletter with information from Orin and DaBen on current earth changes, articles of interest, tape programs, and seminars by Orin and DaBen write: Lumin-Essence Productions, P.O. Box 19117, Oakland, CA 94619; or call (415) 635-1246. Be sure to include your name, address and phone number.

LuminEssence Productions • P.O. Box 19117 • Oakland, CA 94619

Order Form

> BUY ANY THREE TAPES FOR $9.98
> GET A FOURTH $9.98 TAPE FREE!!
> *(Free tape offer does not apply to tape albums.)*

Your Name _____

Address _____

City _____ State _____ Zip _____

Telephone: Home (_____) _____ Work (_____) _____
(In case we have any questions about your order.)

QTY	ITEM	DESCRIPTION	PRICE

POSTAGE RATES:

	First Class Mail*	U.P.S.
Up to $12 ...	$1.45	$2.50
$13 to $25 ...	$2.50	$3.00
$26 to $45 ...	$4.25	$3.50
$46 to 65 ...	$5.75	$4.00
$66 to $85 ...	$7.25	$4.50
$86 to $100 ...	$8.00	$5.75
Over $100 ...	$10.00	$7.00

*For First Class shipping of books
add .50 for each book ordered.

Subtotal	
Sales tax*	
Postage	
Priority handling ($3.00)	
TOTAL	

*CA residents add
appropriate sales tax.

☐ Check here if you prefer your order shipped UPS.
(UPS cannot deliver to PO Box addresses.)

Payment enclosed: ☐ Check ☐ Money Order
Please charge my: ☐ VISA ☐ MasterCard

***Thank You
for
Your Order!***

Credit Card No. _____ Exp. Date _____

Signature as on card _____

Please make check payable to **LuminEssence Productions**. Canadian and foreign orders payable in U.S. Funds. Canadian and Mexican orders add $2.00 to U.S. Postage; other foreign orders add $7.50 to U.S. Postage. All foreign orders will be shipped by air. Regular orders will be shipped within 2 weeks of receipt; priority-handling orders will be shipped within 72 hours of receipt. Remember to allow time for U.S. Mail or UPS delivery after order is shipped. Incomplete orders will be returned.

O5

COMPATIBLE BOOKS FROM

H J KRAMER INC

WAY OF THE PEACEFUL WARRIOR
by Dan Millman
A story of mystery and adventure ideally suited to empower your transformative process. Available in book and audio cassette format.

TALKING WITH NATURE
by Michael J. Roads
A guidebook to align you with the energies of the plant and animal kingdoms.

EAT FOR HEALTH
by William Manahan, M.D.
A loving and compassionate book that will help change eating habits.

JOY IN A WOOLLY COAT
by Julie Adams Church
A simple and inspiring book that provides grief support for pet loss.

JOURNEY INTO NATURE
by Michael J. Roads
A spiritual journey in which you will see humanity through the eyes of nature.

BIOCIRCUITS
by Leslie Patten with Terry Patten
A technology ideally suited for home use, biocircuits can provide you with a direct experience of life force energy.

ANGELS CAN FLY
BECAUSE THEY TAKE THEMSELVES LIGHTLY
by Terry Lynn Taylor with Mary Beth Crain
A light-hearted and practical guide to using angels in your daily life.

YOU THE HEALER
by José Silva and Robert B. Stone
The world-famous Silva Method will teach you to attune to lower-frequency brain waves for use in healing.

LOVE AND PEACE THROUGH AFFIRMATION
by Carole Daxter
Whatever the circumstances of your life, affirmations can help you create a happier, healthier, and more prosperous future.